Middle Level

Six-Way paragraphs

Revised and Expanded

100 Passages for Developing the Six
Essential Categories of Comprehension

Walter Pauk, Ph.D.
Director, Reading Research Center
Cornell University

Jamestown Publishers

Six-Way Paragraphs
Middle Level

Catalog No. 730
© 1983 by Jamestown Publishers, Inc.

Cover design by Deborah Hulsey Christie, adapted from the Original Design by Stephen R. Anthony

Text Design by Deborah Hulsey Christie

Printed in the United States of America
    11 12 BB 98 97

ISBN: 0-89061-302-8

Readability

Passages 1–20:   Level D
Passages 21–40:   Level E
Passages 41–60:   Level F
Passages 61–80:   Level G
Passages 81–100:   Level H

Preface

Learning by Doing

"Please let me do this one by myself." These words echo the age-old principle of learning by doing. And this basic "hands-on" principle works because it makes students *concentrate* and it makes them *think*.

Concentrate. First, to make students concentrate, we compiled stories about what I believe are among the world's most fascinating factual episodes and facts of nature. The stories in this revised and expanded edition of *Six-Way Paragraphs* are all new.

Think. Second, to make students think, we devised six types of questions, which are the only ones that can be legitimately asked about factual prose.

Practice. By answering these six types of questions over and over again, each time in a different context, students learn what to look for when reading factual prose. And once these skills are learned it is easy and natural to carry them over to the reading of textbooks.

In brief, by making students concentrate on factual stories and questions, this book provides a systematic and certain way for teachers to teach and learners to learn.

Acknowledgments

Although I assume complete responsibility for the faults of this book, I am happy to acknowledge my indebtedness to students and colleagues for many of its strong points. The students in all my classes have been helpful in their suggestions and enthusiasm. Graduate students, colleagues and teachers too numerous to mention individually provided criticism when I needed it most. I wish, however, to single out Walter Brownsword, former chairman of the English Department of Community College of Rhode Island, for especial thanks for refining the six-way questions in the first edition. The staff of Jamestown Publishers has been unstintingly helpful in supporting these efforts, through genuine encouragement, and design and editorial assistance in both editions. To all, I am deeply grateful.

Walter Pauk

Ithaca, New York
March 1983

Contents

Titles of Passages

The Paragraph

The paragraph! That's the working-unit of both writer and reader. The writer works hard to put meaning into the paragraph; the reader works hard to take meaning out of it. Though they work at opposite tasks, the work of each is closely related. Actually, to understand better the job of the reader, one must first understand better the job of the writer. So, let us look briefly at the writer's job.

One Main Idea. To make their meaning clear, writers know that they must follow certain basic principles. First, they know that they must develop only one main idea per paragraph. This principle is so important that they know it backward, too. They know that they must not try to develop two main ideas in the same paragraph.

The Topic Sentence. The next important principle they know is that the topic of each main idea must be stated in a topic sentence, and that such a sentence best serves its function by coming at or near the beginning of its paragraph. They know too, that the more clearly they can state the topic of a paragraph in an opening sentence, the more effective they will be in developing a meaningful, well-organized paragraph.

One word of warning to the reader: there is no guarantee that the topic sentence will always be the first sentence of a paragraph. Occasionally, a writer will start off with an introductory or a transitional sentence. Then, it is up to the reader to spot such a sentence, and recognize it for what it is.

The topic sentence may be placed in several other positions in a paragraph. It may be placed in the middle, or even at the very end. If it appears at the end, though it may still be a topic sentence in form, in terms of function, it is more rightfully a *restatement*. Whenever the end position is chosen, it is chosen to give the restatement especial emphasis.

Finally, a paragraph may not have a topic sentence in it at all. Some writers purposely leave out such sentences. But, in such cases, inferring a topic sentence may not be as difficult as it may at first appear. Here's why. Inside information has it that many such professional writers actually do write topic sentences, but on separate scraps of paper. They then place one of the scraps at the head of a sheet and use the topic sentence to guide their thoughts in the construction of the paragraph. With the paragraph written and the topic sentence having served its purpose, the scrap is discarded. The end result is a paragraph without a visible topic sentence, but the paragraph, nonetheless, has embedded in it all the clues that an alert reader needs for making an accurate inference.

Finding Meaning. Actually, there is nothing especially important in recognizing or inferring a topic sentence for its own sake. The important thing is that the reader use the topic sentence as a quick means of establishing a focal point around which to cluster the meanings of the subsequent words and sentences that he or she reads. Here's the double-edged sword again: just as writers use topic sentences to provide focus and structure for presenting their meaning, so the perceptive reader can use the topic sentence for focus and structure to gain meaning.

Up to this point, the reader, having looked secretly over the writer's shoulder, should have learned two exceedingly valuable secrets: first, to always look for only *one* main idea in each paragraph; and secondly, to use the topic sentence to discover the topic of each paragraph.

Supporting the Main Idea. Now, there is more to a writer's job than writing paragraphs that consist of only bare topic sentences and main ideas. The balance of the job deals with *developing* each main idea through the use of supporting material which amplifies and clarifies the main idea and, many times, makes it more vivid and memorable.

To support their main ideas, writers may use a variety of forms. One of the most common is the *example*. Examples help to illustrate the main idea. Other supporting materials are anecdotes, incidents, jokes, allusions, comparisons, contrasts, analogies, definitions, exceptions, logic and so forth.

To summarize, the reader should have learned from the writer that a textbook-type paragraph usually contains these three elements: a topic sentence, a main idea, and supporting material. Knowing this, the reader should use the topic sentence to find the main idea. Everything other than the main idea is supporting material used to illustrate, amplify, and qualify the main idea. So, the reader must be able to separate the main idea from the supporting material, yet see the relationship between them.

To the Instructor

The Reading Passages. Each of the 100 passages included in the book had to meet the following three criteria: *high interest level, appropriate readability level,* and *factual content.*

The high interest level was assured by choosing passages of mature content that would appeal to a wide range of readers.

The readability level of each passage was computed by applying Dr. Edward B. Fry's *Formula for Estimating Readability,* thus enabling the arrangement of passages according to grade levels within the book. *Six-Way Paragraphs, Middle Level* contains passages that range from grade 4 to grade 8 reading level, with twenty passages on each grade level. The passages in *Six-Way Paragraphs, Advanced Level* range from grade 8 to grade 12 readability, with twenty passages on each reading level.

The factual content was a definite requirement because by reading factual passages students build not only their reading skills, but, of equal importance, their informational backgrounds.

The Six Questions. This book is organized around six essential questions. And the bright jewel in this array is the exciting main idea question, which is actually a set of three statements. Students must first choose and label the statement that expresses the *main idea* of the passage, then they must label each of the other statements as being either *too narrow* or *too broad* to be the main idea.

In addition to the main idea question, there are five other questions. These questions are within the framework of the following five categories: subject matter, supporting details, conclusions, clarifying devices, and vocabulary in context.

By repeated practice with the questions within these six categories, students will develop an active, searching attitude that will carry over to the reading of other expository prose. These six types of questions will help them become aware of what they are reading at the time they are actually seeing the words and phrases on a page. This type of thinking-while-reading sets the stage for higher comprehension and better retention.

The Diagnostic Chart. This Diagnostic Chart provides the most dignified form of guidance yet devised. With this Chart, no one has to point out a student's weaknesses. The Chart does that automatically, yielding the information directly and personally to the student, making self-teaching possible. The organization of the questions and the format for marking answers on the Chart are what make it work so well.

The six questions for each passage are always in the same order. For example, the question designed to teach the skill of drawing conclusions is always the fourth question, and the main idea question is always first. This innovation of keeping the questions in a set order sets the stage for the smooth working of the Chart.

The Chart works automatically when the students write the letter of their answer choices for each passage in the spaces provided. Even after completing only one passage, the Chart will reveal the type or types of questions answered correctly, as well as the types answered incorrectly. As the answers for more passages are recorded, the Chart will show the types of questions that are missed consistently. A pattern can be seen after three or more passages have been completed. For example, if a student answers question number four (drawing conclusions) incorrectly for three out of four passages, the student's weakness in this area shows up automatically.

Once a weakness is revealed, have your students take the following steps: First, turn to the instructional pages in the beginning of the book, and study the section in which the topic is discussed. Second, go back and reread the questions that were missed in that particular category. Then, with the correct answer to a question in mind, read the entire passage again, trying to see how the author developed the answer to the question. Do this for each question that was missed. Third, when reading future passages, make an extra effort to correctly answer the questions in that particular category. Fourth, if the difficulty continues, arrange to see the teacher.

To the Student

The Six Types of Questions

In this book, the basic skills necessary for reading factual material are taught through the use of the following six types of questions: *subject matter, main idea, supporting details, conclusion, clarifying devices,* and *vocabulary in context.* Let us take a closer look at each of these types of questions.

Subject Matter. This question looks easy and is easy. But don't let that fool you into thinking it isn't important. It can teach you the most important skill of all reading and learning: concentration. With it, you comprehend and learn. Without it, you fail.

Here's the secret for gaining concentration: After reading the first few lines of something, ask yourself, "What is the subject matter of this passage?" Instantly, you will be thinking about the passage. You will be concentrating.

If you don't ask this question, your eyes will move across the lines of print, yet your mind will be thinking of other things.

By asking this question as you read each passage in this book, you will master the skill so well that it will carry over to everything you read.

Let's see how this method works. Here is a short passage:

> The owl cannot move its eyes. The eyes are fixed in their sockets by strong muscles. But, to make up for this drawback, nature gave the owl a special kind of neck. This neck allows the owl to turn its head in almost a full circle. It can do this without moving the rest of its body.

On finishing the first sentence I hope you said, "Ah, a passage about the owl. Perhaps I'll learn some secret of the wise old bird." If you use this technique, you'll be concentrating, you'll be looking for something, your attitude will be superb, and, best of all, you'll be understanding, learning and remembering.

Main Idea. In reading anything, once you have grasped the subject matter, ask yourself, "What point is the writer trying to make?" Once this question is asked, your mind will be looking for an answer, and chances are that you will find one. But when no question is asked, all things seem equal. Nothing stands out.

Let's try to find the main idea by asking, "What point is the writer trying to make?" in the following passage:

> As an orange tree gets older, its fruit improves. Young trees bear fruit that has a thick rind and many seeds. As the tree becomes older, however, the skins become thinner and the fruit becomes much juicier. The seeds decrease in number. Some old, neglected trees bear fruit with a thin skin and luscious flavor. Some orange trees growing in the Azores bear fruit until they are 100 years old. They produce a highly prized fruit that is thin skinned, full of juice and free from seeds.

I think we'd all agree that a good answer is, "As an orange tree gets older its fruit gets better." In this passage, we were lucky that the first sentence is an excellent *topic sentence*.

The next example does not have a topic sentence to help us. Nevertheless, we'll ask again, "What point is the writer trying to make?" This time, however, you'll have to think about the passage and come up with your own answer.

> Did you ever wonder how much salt is contained in seawater? Here's a simple experiment you might want to try. Take a box six inches deep. Fill it with seawater. Allow the water to evaporate. There will be about two inches of salt left in the bottom of the box. Just think, if all the seawater on the earth evaporated, it would leave a layer of salt about 230 feet thick!

As I said, you had to *think* to come up with an answer. In this case, the answer is a summary type answer. Compare your answer with the following main idea statement: "Seawater has a large amount of salt in it."

Supporting Details. In common usage, the word *detail* has taken on the unrespected meaning of "something relatively unimportant." But details are important. Details are the plaster, board and brick of a building, while main ideas are the large, strong steel or wooden beams. Both are necessary for a solid paragraph.

The bulk of a factual paragraph is made up of details that support the main idea. The main idea is often buried among the details. You have to dig to distinguish between them. Here are some characteristics that can help you see the difference between supporting details and main ideas.

First, supporting details come in various forms, such as examples, explanations, descriptions, definitions, comparisons, contrasts, exceptions, analogies, similes, and metaphors.

Second, these are used to support the main idea. The words themselves, *supporting details*, spell out their job. So, when you have trouble finding the main idea, take the paragraph apart sentence by sentence, asking, "Does this sentence support something, or is this the thing being supported?" In other words, you must not only separate the two, but also see how they help one another. The main idea can often be expressed in a single sentence. But a sentence cannot tell a complete story. The writer must use additional sentences to give you the full picture.

The following passage shows how important details are for providing a full picture of what the writer had in mind.

> Many of the first houses in America were made of bricks taken from ships. Ships, of course, weren't made of brick, but they often carried bricks as ballast. Ballast is heavy material put in the bottom of ships to keep them steady in the water. If a ship is heavier on the top than on the bottom, it is in trouble. The ship will tip over. Many of the ships that came to this country when it was young were almost empty except for bricks and sailors. The sailors knew that they could fill their empty ships with goods from the New World. When the ships arrived in America, their bricks were unloaded and sold. The sailors then had room to put goods from America in the ships' holds in place of the bricks.

Here we have the main idea in one sentence—the first sentence. Having stated the main idea, the writer goes on to explain why the bricks were used in ships and how they ended up being used to build houses. All of the sentences that tell us this information are giving us *supporting details*.

Conclusion. Some paragraphs contain conclusions. Others do not. It all depends on the purpose of the paragraph. For example, some paragraphs describe a process—how something is done. There is no sense in trying to draw a conclusion from such a paragraph. The reader must take it for what it is—a descriptive paragraph.

There are two kinds of paragraphs with conclusions. In one, the conclusion is *stated* by the author. In the other, the conclusion is merely *implied* by the author. That is, the author seems to have come to a conclusion, but has not stated it. It is up to you to draw that conclusion from the paragraph.

Look for the conclusion that is stated in the following paragraph.

> The Earth's atmosphere cuts off all but about 47 percent of the sun's radiation. This is enough to warm our planet but not enough to make it boiling hot. The same heat keeps the earth warm after sunset. The warmth is trapped in the atmosphere, which acts like a blanket to keep us warm. It helps to keep temperatures from falling off too quickly after dark.

The author's conclusion is that the Earth's atmosphere acts like a blanket to keep the planet warm.

In the next excerpt, the author strongly implies a conclusion, but does not state it directly.

> The great enemy of the earthworm is the mole. The pewit bird knows this. In order to make the worms think that a mole is near, the pewit taps the ground with one leg. The worms feel a vibration, or shaking motion, in the earth and think it's a mole. They then make their way to the surface to escape. There the pewit waits to snatch its prey.

From the above excerpt, we can draw the conclusion that the pewit is an intelligent bird.

Looking for a conclusion puts you in the shoes of a detective. While reading, you have to think, "Where is the writer leading me? What's the conclusion?" And, like a detective, you must try to guess the conclusion, changing the guess as you get more and more information.

Clarifying Devices. Clarifying devices are words, phrases and techniques that a writer uses to make main ideas, sub-ideas and supporting details clear and interesting. By knowing some of these clarifying and controlling devices, you will be better able to recognize them in the passages you read. By recognizing them, you will be able to read with greater comprehension and speed.

Similes and Metaphors. Two literary devices that make a writer's ideas both clear and interesting are similes (SIM-a-lees) and metaphors (MET-a-fors). Both are used to make comparisons that add color and power to ideas. An example of a simile is *"She has a mind like a computer."* In this simile, a person's mind is compared to a computer. A simile always uses the word *like, as* or *than* to make a comparison. The metaphor, on the other hand, makes a direct comparison: *"Her mind is a computer."* Because metaphors are shorter and more direct, they are more forceful than similes. Writers use them to capture your attention, touch your emotions, and spark your imagination.

Transitional or Signal Words. The largest single group of clarifying devices, and the most widely used, are transitional or signal words. For example, here are some signal words that you see all the time: *first, second, next, last, finally.* A writer uses such words to keep ideas, steps in a process, or lists in order. Other transitional words include *in brief, in conclusion, above all, therefore, since, because* and *consequently.*

Organizational Patterns. Organizational patterns are also clarifying devices. One such pattern is the *chronological pattern,* in which events unfold in the order of time: one thing happens first, then another, and another, and so on. A time pattern orders events. The event may take place in five minutes or over a period of hundreds of years.

Vocabulary in Context. How accurate are you in using words you think you already know? Do you know that the word *exotic* means "a thing or person from a foreign country?" So, exotic flowers and exotic dancers are flowers and dancers from a foreign country. *Exotic* has been used incorrectly so often and for so long that it has developed a second meaning. Most people use *exotic* to mean "strikingly unusual, as in color or design."

Many people think that the words *imply* and *infer* mean the same thing. They do not. An author may imply, or suggest, something. The reader then infers what the author implied. In other words, to imply is to suggest an idea. To infer is to take meaning out.

It is easy to see what would happen to a passage if a reader skipped a word or two that he or she did not know, and imposed fuzzy meanings on a few others. The result would inevitably be a gross misunderstanding of the author's message. You will become a better reader if you learn the exact meanings and different shades of meaning of the words that are already familiar to you.

Answering the Main Idea Question

The main idea questions in this book are not the usual multiple-choice variety from which you must select the one correct statement. Rather, you are given three statements and are asked to select the statement that expresses the *main idea* of the passage, the statement that is *too narrow,* and the statement that is *too broad.* You have to work hard and actively to identify all three statements correctly. This new type of question teaches you the differences among statements that, at first, seem almost equal.

To help you handle these questions, let's go behind the scenes to see how the main idea questions in this book were constructed. The true main idea statement was always written first. It had to be neat, succinct and positive. The main idea tells *who* or *what* the subject of the passage is. It also answers the question *does what?* or *is what?* Next, keeping the main idea statement in mind, the other two statements were written. They are variations of the main idea statement. The *too narrow* statement had to be in line with the main idea, but express only part of it. Likewise, the *too broad* statement had to be in line with the main idea, but be too general in scope.

Read the sample passage that starts below. Then follow the instructions in the box, to learn how to answer the main idea questions. The answer to each part of the question has been filled in for you. The score for each answer has also been marked.

Sample Passage
Silk is fancy cloth that is much softer than cotton. Silk is made by the silkworm caterpillar. When full grown, the caterpillar weaves a cocoon of silk strands. It makes a sticky gum to hold the threads together. Long

ago, in ancient China, people discovered how to wash the gum away. This made it possible for them to unwind the silk threads and weave them into cloth. The shimmering fabric could be dyed many colors. The process of making silk fabric was a Chinese secret for 2000 years. The Chinese sold silk to the rest of the world. But silkworms were eventually smuggled out of China. Now silk is made in many places around the world. The tiny silkworm is now part of a big industry.

1

	Answer	Score
Mark the *main idea* →	**M**	15
Mark the statement that is *too broad* →	**B**	5
Mark the statement that is *too narrow* →	**N**	5

a. Silkworms make silk thread that can be woven into beautiful cloth.   M   15

[This statement is the main idea. It gathers all the important points of the passage. It tells (1) that the passage is about the silkworm, (2) that the silkworm makes silk thread, and (3) that it is woven into beautiful cloth.]

b. Silkworms make silk.   B   5

[This statement is too broad. Although the sentence is true, it leaves out some important points. We don't know (1) what form the silk takes when it is made, or (2) what the silk is used for.]

c. Silkworms spin silk cocoons.   N   5

[This sentence is too narrow. It tells us only part of the story. It completely ignores the fact that the silkworm's silk is made into cloth.]

Getting the Most Out of This Book

The following steps could be called "tricks of the trade." Your teachers might call them "rules for learning." It doesn't matter what they are called. What does matter is that they work.

Think About the Title. A famous language expert told me a "trick" to use when I read. "The first thing to do is to read the title. Then spend a few moments thinking about it."

Writers spend much time thinking up good titles. They try to pack a lot of meaning into them. It makes sense, then, for you to spend a few seconds trying to dig out some meaning. These few moments of thought will give you a head start on a passage.

Thinking about the title can help you in another way, too. It helps you concentrate on a passage before you begin reading. Why does this happen? Thinking about the title fills your head full of thoughts about the passage. There's no room for anything else to get in to break concentration.

The Dot System. Here is a method that will speed up your reading. It also builds comprehension at the same time.

Spend a few moments with the title. Then read *quickly* through the passage. Next, without looking back, answer the six questions by placing a dot in the box next to each answer of your choice. The dots will be your "unofficial" answers. For the main idea question (question one), place your dot in the box next to the statement that you think is the main idea.

The dot system helps by making you think hard on your first, *fast* reading. The practice you gain by trying to grasp and remember ideas makes you a stronger reader.

The Check-Mark System. First, answer the main idea question. Follow the steps that are given above each set of statements for this question. Use a capital letter to mark your final answer to each part of the main idea question.

You have answered the other five questions with a dot. Now read the passage once more *carefully*. This time, mark your final answer to each question by placing a check mark (✔) in the box next to the answer of your choice. The answers with the check marks are the ones that will count toward your score.

The Diagnostic Chart. Now move your final answers to the Diagnostic Chart that starts on page 230.

Use the row of boxes beside *Passage 1* for the answers to the first passage. Use the row of boxes beside *Passage 2* for the answers to the second passage, and so on.

Write the letter of your answer to the left of the dotted line in each block.

Correct your answers using the Answer Key on pages 225–229. When scoring your answers, do *not* use an *x* for *incorrect* or a *c* for *correct*. Instead, use this method. If your choice is correct, make no mark in the right side of the answer block. If your choice is *incorrect*, write the letter of the correct answer to the right of the dotted line in the block.

Thus, the row of answers for each passage will show your incorrect answers. And it will also show the correct answers.

Your Total Comprehension Score. Go back to the passage you have just read. If you answered a question incorrectly, draw a line under the correct choice on the question page. Then write your score for each question on the line provided. Add the scores to get your total comprehension score. Enter that number in the box marked Total Score.

Graphing Your Progress. After you have found your total comprehension score, turn to the Progress Graph that begins on page 235. Write your score in the box under the number for the passage. Then put an **x** along the line above the box to show your total comprehension score. Join the **x**'s as you go. This will plot a line showing your progress.

Taking Corrective Action. Your incorrect answers give you a way to teach yourself how to read better. Take the time to study your wrong answers.

Go back to the questions. For each question you got wrong, read the correct answer (the one you have underlined) several times. With the correct answer in mind, go back to the passage itself. Read to see why the approved answer is better. Try to see where you made your mistake. Try to figure out why you chose a wrong answer.

The Steps in a Nutshell

Here's a quick review of the steps to follow. Following these steps is the way to get the most out of this book. Be sure you have read and understood all of the "To the Student" section on pages 13 through 21 before you start.

1. **Think About the Title of the Passage.** Try to get all the meaning the writer put into it.

2. **Read the Passage Quickly.**

3. **Answer the Questions, Using the Dot System.** Use dots to mark your unofficial answers. Don't look back at the passage.

4. **Read the Passage Again—Carefully.**

5. **Mark Your Final Answers.** Put a check mark (✓) in the box to note your final answer. Use capital letters for each part of the main idea question.

6. **Mark Your Answers on the Diagnostic Chart.** Record your final answers in the Diagnostic Chart that begins on page 230. Write your answers to the left of the dotted line in the answer blocks for the passage.

7. **Correct Your Answers.** Use the Answer Key on pages 225–229. If an answer is not correct, write the correct answer in the right side of the block, beside your wrong answer. Then go back to the question page. Place a line under the correct answer.

8. **Find Your Total Comprehension Score.** Find this by adding up the points you earned for each question. Enter the total in the box marked Total Score.

9. **Graph Your Progress.** Enter and plot your score on the graph that begins on page 235.

10. **Take Corrective Action.** Read your wrong answers. Read the passage once more. Try to figure out why you were wrong.

Joker's Wild

Watch out for practical jokers. They'll do almost anything for a laugh.
One such prankster was Moe Drabowsky. He was a baseball relief
pitcher. Relief pitchers are standby players who replace the starting
pitcher in a game if he is pitching badly. If the starting pitcher is throw-
ing well, relief pitchers have nothing to do. They just sit around in the
bullpen and hope the manager calls them to play.

Waiting around in the bullpen gave Moe lots of time to think up
jokes. But his best joke was played after he retired from baseball. Moe was
sitting at home watching his team play on television. It would have been
a boring game for him had he still been on the team. The starting pitcher
was doing great. He hadn't given up a single run. The relief pitchers
wouldn't be likely to play in this game. The last thing they'd expect
would be a call from the manager. The thought gave Moe a mischievous
idea. He still remembered the bullpen phone number. Moe dialed it from
his living room. A startled relief pitcher answered. Using a voice that
sounded like the manager's, Moe growled, "Warm up and get ready
to play." The star pitcher <u>gaped</u> at the man in the bullpen who was
getting ready to pitch. Everyone stared at the manager in disbelief. The
poor manager could only scratch his head. A thousand miles away,
Moe Drabowsky sat in his living room watching the event on TV
and laughing.

Main Idea	1		Answer	Score
		Mark the *main idea* ⟶	M	15
		Mark the statement that is *too broad* ⟶	B	5
		Mark the statement that is *too narrow* ⟶	N	5

a. Moe Drabowsky played a great
practical joke on his team after he
retired from baseball. ☐ _____

b. Relief pitchers spend a lot of time
waiting in the bullpen. ☐ _____

c. Moe Drabowsky played a lot of
practical jokes. ☐ _____

Subject Matter

2 This passage is concerned with

- [ ] a. a baseball game.
- [ ] b. a practical joke.
- [ ] c. advice on pitching.
- [ ] d. a TV show.

_____

Supporting Details

3 The relief pitcher who answered the phone in the bullpen thought he was talking to

- [ ] a. the President.
- [ ] b. his manager.
- [ ] c. Moe.
- [ ] d. the phone company.

_____

Conclusion

4 We can assume that Moe made the call

- [ ] a. because he was jealous of the successful pitchers.
- [ ] b. from a phone booth.
- [ ] c. long distance.
- [ ] d. during the winter.

_____

Clarifying Devices

5 This passage

- [ ] a. makes fun of baseball players.
- [ ] b. tells you how to play practical jokes on people.
- [ ] c. teaches a lesson.
- [ ] d. tells an amusing story.

_____

Vocabulary in Context

6 In this passage the word <u>gaped</u> means

- [ ] a. yelled.
- [ ] b. glanced.
- [ ] c. stared with open mouth.
- [ ] d. waved.

_____

Add your scores for questions 1–6. Enter the total here and on the graph on page 235.

Total Score [ ]

A Dragon That Flies

Although it doesn't breathe fire, this dragon can fly. And what a beauty it is! By far the scariest thing about the dragonfly is its name. This double-winged, fast flying insect is totally harmless. It has large, deep eyes that can detect the smallest movements. Its body may be bright blue and red, or vivid green. Dragonflies in flight look like dancing spots of color in the light of a midsummer's day.

The dragonfly has a long and respectable history. It was one of the first flying insects on earth. To see this sage of the insect world in action, head for a pond. Dragonflies live near the water. In fact, they lay their eggs right in the water. A dragonfly egg goes through several big changes before it becomes a flying insect. From the egg, a tiny creature called a nymph is hatched. It lives in the water, eating other small creatures that live in the pond. As the nymph grows, it becomes too big for its skin. It sheds the skin that is too small for it and grows a new one. This <u>molting</u> happens several times, until the insect is full grown. Then it crawls up the stem of a water plant, out into the air. It squeezes its way out of its last skin as a full-fledged dragonfly.

After going through all that work to grow up, the dragonfly only lives for about a month. But, for this short time, it startles the hot summer air with its bright beauty.

Main Idea	1		Answer	Score
		Mark the *main idea* ———→	M	15
		Mark the statement that is *too broad* ———→	B	5
		Mark the statement that is *too narrow* ———→	N	5

a. Dragonflies are harmless, beautiful insects with an interesting life cycle. ☐ _____

b. Dragonflies live and breed near ponds. ☐ _____

c. Insects that live near water are harmless and fascinating. ☐ _____

Subject Matter

2 This passage is mostly about
- ☐ a. fire-breathing dragons.
- ☐ b. dragonflies.
- ☐ c. pond life.
- ☐ d. flying insects.   _____

Supporting Details

3 Young dragonfly nymphs eat
- ☐ a. flies.
- ☐ b. their eggs.
- ☐ c. pond vegetation.
- ☐ d. other pond creatures.   _____

Conclusion

4 We can conclude that dragonflies are
- ☐ a. frightening to look at.
- ☐ b. good swimmers.
- ☐ c. only make believe.
- ☐ d. ancient creatures.   _____

Clarifying Devices

5 In the last sentence, the author refers to
- ☐ a. the speed of the dragonfly.
- ☐ b. the viciousness of the dragonfly.
- ☐ c. the loveliness of the dragonfly.
- ☐ d. the wings of the dragonfly.   _____

Vocabulary in Context

6 Molting means
- ☐ a. swimming.
- ☐ b. shedding skin.
- ☐ c. growing.
- ☐ d. nymph stage.   _____

Add your scores for questions 1–6. Enter the total here and on the graph on page 235.

Total
Score [   ]

Sea Turtles

Did you know that a turtle can lay twelve eggs in one minute? A large sea turtle lays around 150 eggs at a time. She lays all these eggs in just a few minutes.

Large sea turtles live in the warm seas of the world. Except for when they lay their eggs, they spend their whole lives in water. When it is time to lay their eggs, the females swim to land. They usually return to the place where they themselves were born. How they find their way back there is a mystery.

When they reach shore, the big, heavy turtles crawl slowly up to the high water mark. Using their flippers, they pull themselves along the sand. They must struggle like mountain climbers to attain their goal. When they finally reach dry sand, they rest before beginning the difficult task of laying eggs.

The turtles lay the eggs in deep holes and cover them with warm sand. The sand protects the eggs from harm. Then the females leave them. After a few weeks, if you happened to be walking along the beach, you might see the sand begin to shake in one spot. Then you would see tiny black balls coming out of the sand. The tiny heads of baby turtles!

Baby turtles have a built-in sense of direction. As soon as they are hatched, they head for the water. Once the babies swim out to sea, they don't touch shore again until it is time for them to lay their own eggs.

Main Idea	1		Answer	Score
		Mark the *main idea* ⟶	M	15
		Mark the statement that is *too broad* ⟶	B	5
		Mark the statement that is *too narrow* ⟶	N	5
		a. Sea turtles have fascinating life habits.	☐	___
		b. Sea turtles swim to shore to lay their eggs.	☐	___
		c. Large sea turtles lay their eggs in special ways.	☐	___

Subject Matter **2** The first sentence lets us know that this passage is about

☐ a. turtles.
☐ b. oceans.
☐ c. time.
☐ d. eggs.

_____

Supporting Details **3** Turtles bury their eggs

☐ a. to keep them cool.
☐ b. to protect them from danger.
☐ c. because of deep instinct.
☐ d. to protect them from the weather.

_____

Conclusion **4** We can conclude from this passage that

☐ a. many turtles die while swimming to shore.
☐ b. female turtles protect their babies.
☐ c. once turtles land, they never return to the sea.
☐ d. the job of laying eggs takes tremendous strength.

_____

Clarifying Devices **5** The writer compares turtles to mountain climbers

☐ a. because they lay their eggs in mountain areas.
☐ b. to give you a picture of how hard they work.
☐ c. to tell you that they like to climb.
☐ d. to tell you that mountain climbers are as slow as turtles.

_____

Vocabulary in Context **6** In this passage, the word <u>attain</u> means

☐ a. see.
☐ b. push.
☐ c. bury.
☐ d. reach.

_____

Add your scores for questions 1-6. Enter the total here and on the graph on page 235.   **Total Score** ☐

4

Birds Like to be Clean, Too!

Imagine taking a dust bath to keep clean! Sparrows have to bathe in dust to keep pests out of their feathers. Tiny bugs such as fleas and lice can be a problem for birds. In órder to keep these pests away, birds preen themselves. Preening is just a fancy name for keeping clean. Birds preen by running their beaks through their feathers. The beak acts like a tiny comb, picking up dirt, bits of leaves and pesty bugs.

A bird called the starling has the most <u>remarkable</u> way of keeping its feathers tidy. It uses ants! A starling covers its wings with ants. The ants gobble up insect pests that hide among the starling's feathers.

Most birds like to dip into a lake or a puddle of water to wash off. They splash around like toddlers in a pool, hopping first on one leg, then on the other. Birds like to have fun while washing up too!

			Answer	Score
Main Idea	**1**			
		Mark the *main idea* ⟶	M	15
		Mark the statement that is *too broad* ⟶	B	5
		Mark the statement that is *too narrow* ⟶	N	5

a. Birds have many ways of keeping clean. ☐ ____

b. Birds have many interesting habits. ☐ ____

c. Sparrows bathe in dust to keep bugs out of their feathers. ☐ ____

Score 15 points for each correct answer. **Score**

Subject Matter

2 This passage deals mostly with

- ☐ a. how birds lay eggs.
- ☐ b. how birds keep clean.
- ☐ c. birds that like water.
- ☐ d. birds that eat bugs. _____

Supporting Details

3 Ants help the starling to

- ☐ a. keep clean.
- ☐ b. find food.
- ☐ c. build its nest.
- ☐ d. keep its feathers dry. _____

Conclusion

4 After reading this passage, we can see that

- ☐ a. all birds love water.
- ☐ b. birds get very dirty.
- ☐ c. staying clean is important to birds.
- ☐ d. preening takes a lot of time. _____

Clarifying Devices

5 The writer thinks that birds bathing in a lake or puddle are

- ☐ a. nervous.
- ☐ b. preening.
- ☐ c. having a good time.
- ☐ d. very clean. _____

Vocabulary in Context

6 Remarkable means

- ☐ a. talked about.
- ☐ b. helpful.
- ☐ c. unusual.
- ☐ d. best. _____

Add your scores for questions 1-6. Enter the total here and on the graph on page 235.

Total Score ☐

31

Six-Legged Workers

Can you imagine being able to lift fifty people at once and carry them? You'd have to have superhuman strength. Well, you may be surprised to know that tiny ants do have this kind of strength. An ant can lift a load fifty times heavier than itself! Ants must often carry food to their homes from places that are far away. To do this, they must be very strong.

Ants live in tunnels that twist and turn in many directions, like the roots of a gnarled old tree. Thousands of ants can live in one nest. The tunnels are divided into parts. Each part serves a special purpose.

The royal chamber is the place where the queen ant lays her eggs. The queen spends her whole life laying eggs. She never leaves her chamber, except to start a new nest. Worker ants must bring food to her.

The worker ants in an ant colony have many different jobs. Some workers pull the eggs from the royal chamber into a room called the "nursery." There, they help larvae climb out of their shells. Larvae are the baby ants when they first come out of the eggs. In the nursery, there are workers who look after the larvae until they become full-grown ants. Some workers look for food and store it in the granary, where seeds are kept. Others dump leftovers in the rubbish room. Ants have their own complete, busy world hidden in tunnels under our feet!

Main Idea	1		Answer	Score
	Mark the *main idea* ⟶	M		15
	Mark the statement that is *too broad* ⟶	B		5
	Mark the statement that is *too narrow* ⟶	N		5

a. In an ant colony, the ants have many different jobs. ☐ _____

b. Ants are very busy insects. ☐ _____

c. An ant can carry fifty times its own weight. ☐ _____

Score 15 points for each correct answer.   **Score**

**Subject
Matter**

2 This passage is mostly about

☐ a. human strength.

☐ b. ants at work.

☐ c. gnarled old trees.

☐ d. food storage.   _____

**Supporting
Details**

3 In the nursery, worker ants look after the

☐ a. queen.

☐ b. seeds.

☐ c. larvae.

☐ d. leftovers.   _____

Conclusion

4 Dividing the work so that each worker has a certain
job helps

☐ a. keep the nest organized.

☐ b. the queen to get more food.

☐ c. keep the workers happy.

☐ d. the ants live longer.   _____

**Clarifying
Devices**

5 The writer compares the twisting tunnels of an
ant nest to

☐ a. the strength of humans.

☐ b. a gnarled old tree.

☐ c. a royal palace.

☐ d. a hospital nursery.   _____

**Vocabulary
in Context**

6 The word <u>gnarled</u> means

☐ a. twisted.

☐ b. giant.

☐ c. confusing.

☐ d. difficult.   _____

**Add your scores for questions 1-6. Enter the
total here and on the graph on page 235.**

**Total
Score** ☐

Bear Facts

What do bears like to eat besides honey? They enjoy all sorts of things, such as fish, berries, and even roots. But their favorite foods are sweet. That's why they raid bees' nests for dessert. A fierce grizzly, which can weigh as much as ten men, can be made happy with a piece of sweet fruit.

Did you ever wonder what kind of bears appear in fairy tales? They are European brown bears. Though hundreds of brown bears once inhabited the forests of Europe, today there are hardly any left. Brown bears are relatives of the Kodiak and grizzly bears of North America.

Polar bears live in the coldest parts of the world. Did you know that they spend half of their lives in water? The polar bear is an excellent diver and swimmer. It can close its nostrils and swim below the surface for as long as two minutes. The polar bear's hind legs act as a rudder to direct its movements. Since there are no bees' nests or fruits in icy lands, the polar bear must search for other foods. It wanders for hours over the frozen ocean, looking for breathing holes made by seals. When it finds one, it cracks the ice with its huge paws. Then it waits for the seal to peek out. As soon as the seal's head is above the ice, the bear swings one of its mighty paws and jerks the seal out of the water. Then one more blow, and the bear has a feast of seal meat.

Main Idea	1		Answer	Score
	Mark the *main idea* ⟶	M		15
	Mark the statement that is *too broad* ⟶	B		5
	Mark the statement that is *too narrow* ⟶	N		5

a. Most bears eat honey and fruit. ☐ _____

b. There are many different kinds of bears. ☐ _____

c. There are many animals in the world. ☐ _____

Score 15 points for each correct answer.   **Score**

**Subject
Matter**
2 This passage focuses on
   ☐ a. fruits and honey.
   ☐ b. fairy tales.
   ☐ c. bears.
   ☐ d. European forests.   _____

**Supporting
Details**
3 The bears in fairy tales are
   ☐ a. grizzly bears.
   ☐ b. Kodiak bears.
   ☐ c. polar bears.
   ☐ d. European brown bears.   _____

Conclusion
4 You would <u>not</u> expect to find a polar bear in
   ☐ a. South America.
   ☐ b. Alaska.
   ☐ c. the Arctic.
   ☐ d. the North Pole.   _____

**Clarifying
Devices**
5 The author develops the main idea by means of
   ☐ a. contrast.
   ☐ b. definitions.
   ☐ c. examples.
   ☐ d. argument.   _____

**Vocabulary
in Context**
6 In this passage, the word <u>blow</u> means
   ☐ a. to destroy by explosion.
   ☐ b. a sudden hard hit.
   ☐ c. a terrible shock.
   ☐ d. to force air against something.   _____

**Add your scores for questions 1-6. Enter the
total here and on the graph on page 235.**

**Total
Score** ☐

7

The Whale Clan

If you're looking for a whale you have a whole family of creatures to choose from. The papa of the whale family is, of course, the whale itself. But there are other members as well. Relatives, you might say.

Few people realize that dolphins are part of the whale clan. In fact, many people do not realize that dolphins aren't fish. Fish breathe through gills and lay eggs. The dolphin does neither. Dolphins, like all the members of the whale clan, are mammals. They breathe air and they have babies like land mammals, and feed them with milk. Dolphins are fascinating to watch. They can leap high out of the water and perform turns in the air. These leaps give the dolphin time to breathe.

Porpoises also belong to the whale family and are very much like dolphins. The main difference between dolphins and porpoises is the size and shape of the snout. The dolphin's nose is long and thin. The snout of the porpoise is short and stubby. Both creatures are smart and friendly to humans.

Not all the members of the family are friendly. Perhaps the difference in mood has to do with size. The giant whale is much grumpier than the smaller dolphin or porpoise. An angry whale can be hard to ignore. Perhaps this <u>trait</u> helped to inspire the story of Moby Dick, the Great White Whale who sank a ship and caused the crew to drown?

Main Idea   1

	Answer	Score
Mark the *main idea* ⟶	M	15
Mark the statement that is *too broad* ⟶	B	5
Mark the statement that is *too narrow* ⟶	N	5

a. Like whales, dolphins are mammals. ☐ _____

b. An animal family is made up of many different kinds of animals. ☐ _____

c. Dolphins, porpoises and whales are all part of the same family. ☐ _____

Score 15 points for each correct answer.   Score

Subject Matter   **2** This passage is mostly about
☐ a. the food whales eat.
☐ b. three members of the whale family.
☐ c. the difference between dolphins and porpoises.
☐ d. Moby Dick.
_____

Supporting Details   **3** All members of the whale family breathe air because they're
☐ a. related.
☐ b. talented.
☐ c. mammals.
☐ d. fish.
_____

Conclusion   **4** We can conclude that
☐ a. porpoises breathe air and feed their babies milk.
☐ b. porpoises are much larger than dolphins.
☐ c. porpoises avoid human beings.
☐ d. porpoises do not leap out of the water.
_____

Clarifying Devices   **5** Calling porpoises and dolphins "relatives" of the whale means
☐ a. they are related by marriage.
☐ b. they belong to the same mammal family.
☐ c. they are born from whales.
☐ d. they live in the same area as whales.
_____

Vocabulary in Context   **6** In this passage the word <u>trait</u> means
☐ a. fear.
☐ b. mammal.
☐ c. anger.
☐ d. characteristic.
_____

Add your scores for questions 1-6. Enter the total here and on the graph on page 235.   Total Score ☐

8

The Busy Bees

In addition to being a great honey maker, the bee is a wonderful dancer! When a honeybee finds a new patch of flowers, it returns to the hive and performs a special dance for the other bees. This dance tells the other bees where the flowers are. If the flowers are nearby, the bee dances in a circle. If they are farther away, it dances in a figure eight. If the bee circles upward, the flowers are in the same direction as the sun.

The message dance is one way in which bees help each other. Thousands of honeybees may live in one nest. In order to keep things running smoothly, the bees must cooperate with each other. Every bee in a hive has a certain job to do. The queen bee lays the eggs. She may lay up to two thousand eggs in one day! Each hive has only one queen. Worker bees must gather pollen and nectar for food. They store nectar in the cells of the hive. Then they turn the nectar into honey.

Workers also build the hives. They shape wax into hundreds of tiny six-sided cells called honeycombs. A bee can make wax inside its own body! The wax flows out of tiny holes in the abdomen. The bee chews the wax until it is soft enough to mold.

Main Idea 1

	Answer	Score
Mark the *main idea* ⟶	M	15
Mark the statement that is *too broad* ⟶	B	5
Mark the statement that is *too narrow* ⟶	N	5

a. Worker bees build honeycombs from wax that is made inside their bodies. ☐ _____

b. Bees are hardworking insects. ☐ _____

c. Bees work together to keep their hive running smoothly. ☐ _____

Score 15 points for each correct answer.

**Subject
Matter**

2 Another good title for this passage would be
- ☐ a. Pollen Counts.
- ☐ b. How to Make Honey.
- ☐ c. Working Together.
- ☐ d. The Message Dance.

_____

**Supporting
Details**

3 The message dance tells other bees
- ☐ a. where flowers are located.
- ☐ b. how large the flower patch is.
- ☐ c. where to find honey.
- ☐ d. how good the pollen is.

_____

Conclusion

4 It is clear from this passage that the author admires
- ☐ a. the hard work of the bees.
- ☐ b. the ways in which bees work together.
- ☐ c. the way bees gather pollen and nectar.
- ☐ d. the strength of the queen bee.

_____

**Clarifying
Devices**

5 The purpose of the first sentence in this passage is to
- ☐ a. jog your memory.
- ☐ b. awaken your feelings.
- ☐ c. get your attention.
- ☐ d. put you in a good mood.

_____

**Vocabulary
in Context**

6 As used in the second paragraph, the word cooperate means
- ☐ a. make honey.
- ☐ b. work together.
- ☐ c. fly in groups.
- ☐ d. dance in circles.

_____

**Add your scores for questions 1–6. Enter the
total here and on the graph on page 235.**

Total
Score

9

Rain Forests

Tropical rain forests grow near the equator, in the hottest parts of the world. Rain forests are always wet. The moisture just never dries up.

The trees in a rain forest are very tall and have very few limbs. The leaves are all at the top. They form a high ceiling. Very little sunlight comes through the leaves. Inside a rain forest it is as dark and quiet as a church.

There are very few low growing plants on the rain forest floor. Walking through a rain forest is like being at a circus's high trapeze show—the most exciting things are happening high above the ground. Monkeys swing on vines, with baby monkeys on their backs. Large snakes crawl from branch to branch. Giant bats make squeaky noises.

The animals that stay near the ground are <u>fascinating</u> too. The gentle tapir, which looks like a small horse with a long nose, covers itself with mud from head to foot. When the mud dries, it forms a kind of armor. It protects the tapir from biting insects. Another ground animal is the anteater. It has a long, sticky tongue that works like a fly trap. But it's really an ant trap. For breakfast, lunch and dinner it eats nothing but ants, ants, and more ants!

Main Idea 1

	Answer	Score
Mark the *main idea* ⟶	M	15
Mark the statement that is *too broad* ⟶	B	5
Mark the statement that is *too narrow* ⟶	N	5

a. Rain forests are hot and wet. ☐ _____

b. A rain forest is a home for many interesting animals. ☐ _____

c. Many interesting animals live in tropical climates. ☐ _____

Subject Matter **2** This passage is mainly about

☐ a. trees.

☐ b. tropical rain forests.

☐ c. anteaters.

☐ d. monkeys. _____

Supporting Details **3** Mud protects the tapir from

☐ a. monkeys.

☐ b. anteaters.

☐ c. the heat.

☐ d. biting insects. _____

Conclusion 4 It is probable that few plants grow on the rain forest floor because

☐ a. there is not enough light.

☐ b. most animals are in the trees.

☐ c. there is not enough water.

☐ d. it is too hot. _____

Clarifying Devices **5** The activity in a rain forest is compared to

☐ a. a zoo.

☐ b. a church.

☐ c. a circus trapeze show.

☐ d. a tropical pet shop. _____

Vocabulary in Context **6** A fascinating animal is

☐ a. dangerous.

☐ b. interesting.

☐ c. frightening.

☐ d. active. _____

Add your scores for questions 1-6. Enter the total here and on the graph on page 235.

Total Score ☐

Two Unhappy Firsts

10

People enjoy talking about "firsts." They like to remember their first love or their first car. But not all firsts are happy ones. Few people enjoy recalling the firsts that are bad.

One of history's bad but important firsts was the first car accident. Autos were still young when it happened. The crash took place in New York City. The year was 1896. The month was May. A man from Massachusetts was visiting the city in his new car. At the time, bicycle riders were still trying to get used to the new set of wheels on the road. No one is sure who was at fault. In any case, the bike and the car collided. The man on the bike was injured. The driver of the car had to stay in jail and wait for the hospital report on the bicycle rider. Luckily, the rider was not killed.

Three years later, another automobile first took place. The scene was again New York City. A real estate broker named Henry Bliss stepped off a streetcar. He was hit by a passing car. Once again, no one is sure just how it happened or whose fault it was. The driver of the car was put in jail. Poor Mr. Bliss became the first person to die in a car accident.

Main Idea 1

	Answer	Score
Mark the *main idea*	M	15
Mark the statement that is *too broad*	B	5
Mark the statement that is *too narrow*	N	5

a. Not all firsts are happy firsts. ☐ _____

b. The first car accident and the first death from a car accident are two very unhappy "firsts." ☐ _____

c. It took bicycle riders a while to get used to cars on the road. ☐ _____

Score 15 points for each correct answer.   Score

Subject Matter   **2** This passage is about

☐ a. the first bicycle accident.

☐ b. accidents in large cities.

☐ c. two of the first auto accidents.

☐ d. the first vehicles with wheels.   _____

Supporting Details   **3** In each accident the driver was

☐ a. found guilty.

☐ b. set free.

☐ c. laughed at.

☐ d. put in jail for a while.   _____

Conclusion   **4** We can conclude that accidents involving cars

☐ a. happened most often in New York City.

☐ b. do not happen as often as they did in the early days of the auto.

☐ c. have killed many more people since Mister Bliss was killed.

☐ d. were always the driver's fault.   _____

Clarifying Devices   **5** The "new set of wheels" that bicycle riders had to get used to was

☐ a. the new tires on their bikes.

☐ b. the automobile.

☐ c. the streetcar.

☐ d. the bicycle itself.   _____

Vocabulary in Context   **6** <u>Collided</u> means

☐ a. hit each other hard.

☐ b. stopped.

☐ c. raced each other.

☐ d. traveled in the same direction.   _____

Add your scores for questions 1-6. Enter the total here and on the graph on page 235.   Total Score ☐

11

Insects with Hard Hats

Imagine never being able to stoop down and touch your toes! Beetles can't ever bend over. Their bodies are covered with a very stiff, hard coat that protects their soft insides. If a beetle falls on its back, it can't get up again. Like a knight who has fallen off his horse, the insect is pinned to the ground by its heavy armor.

Only the click beetle can jump right up without help. What is the click beetle's special secret? It has a peg hidden near its front legs. The peg works like a spring. When the beetle falls, the spring lets go. The insect is thrown high up into the air. It turns in the air, and then comes down on its feet. The name "click beetle" comes from the sound that the spring makes.

There are hundreds of varieties of beetles. Some are a big help to people. Take the ladybug for example. These little red bugs sprinkled with black dots work for us day and night. They eat insects that kill plants. So, if you see a ladybug crawling over your plants, don't kill it!

But not all beetles are as helpful as ladybugs. Some are just a bother. For example, the deathwatch beetle loves to explore old buildings. It creeps and crawls inside hollow walls. It makes an eerie sound by tapping on the wood with its head. When people hear these noises, but don't know what's causing them, they become alarmed. But the beetle does not mean to be frightening. It is just trying to call its mate.

Main Idea	1		Answer	Score
		Mark the *main idea* ⟶	M	15
		Mark the statement that is *too broad* ⟶	B	5
		Mark the statement that is *too narrow* ⟶	N	5
		a. Beetles can be helpful to people.	☐	_____
		b. The insect world is very interesting and varied.	☐	_____
		c. There are many interesting kinds of beetles.	☐	_____

Score 15 points for each correct answer.   **Score**

Subject **2** This passage focuses on
Matter
    ☐ a. knights.
    ☐ b. exercise.
    ☐ c. beetles.
    ☐ d. insects.   _____

Supporting **3** The ladybug is helpful to people because it
Details
    ☐ a. eats insects that kill plants.
    ☐ b. eats harmful plants.
    ☐ c. is not poisonous.
    ☐ d. brightens up the garden.   _____

Conclusion **4** The deathwatch beetle calls its mate by
    ☐ a. performing a special dance.
    ☐ b. flying in circles.
    ☐ c. crawling inside walls.
    ☐ d. tapping on wood.   _____

Clarifying **5** The fifth sentence compares the beetle to
Devices
    ☐ a. a soldier.
    ☐ b. a horse.
    ☐ c. a suit of armor.
    ☐ d. a knight.   _____

Vocabulary **6** In this passage, <u>alarmed</u> means
in Context
    ☐ a. watchful.
    ☐ b. frightened.
    ☐ c. curious.
    ☐ d. attentive.   _____

Add your scores for questions 1-6. Enter the   Total
total here and on the graph on page 235.   Score

12

Birds Among Buildings

Where can you find huge nests perched on chimneys? In some countries in Europe, storks build their homes on rooftops. They work for days to build a nest. They pick up large sticks with their beaks. Then they fly high into the air and balance their sticks on the huge, windy chimneys. Anyone watching from below is happy to see these visitors arrive. People believe that storks bring good luck.

Many birds live in cities and enjoy the company of people. Often, birds that make their nests in rocky places think the tall city buildings are cliffs. Wild pigeons, for example, live on rocky hills. City pigeons build their nests on window ledges.

Some birds come to towns to sleep because it is too cold in the country. They often look for places where warm air comes from a building. And what could be warmer than a chimney? Birds called chimney swifts sleep in the smokestacks of old factories. Just before dark, a flock of swifts will <u>hover</u> above a chimney. Then the birds fly in a circle, entering the chimney one by one. Their spiral flight looks like water swirling down a pipe. As night falls, the swifts cling to the chimney walls, warm and safe.

Main Idea	1		Answer	Score
	Mark the *main idea* ⟶	**M**	15
	Mark the statement that is *too broad* ⟶	**B**	5
	Mark the statement that is *too narrow* ⟶	**N**	5

a. Many birds live in cities. ☐ _____

b. Birds live in many different kinds of places. ☐ _____

c. Some birds like to live on chimneys. ☐ _____

Score 15 points for each correct answer.   Score

Subject Matter   **2** This passage is mostly concerned with

☐ a. buildings in cities.
☐ b. rocky ledges.
☐ c. birds in towns and cities.
☐ d. birds of the country.   _____

Supporting Details   **3** Why do some birds come to towns to sleep?

☐ a. It is too cold in the country.
☐ b. It is too quiet in the country.
☐ c. Birds like high rooftops.
☐ d. Birds like the ledges of buildings.   _____

Conclusion   **4** Birds probably like to live around people because they

☐ a. like the sound of human voices.
☐ b. know they will find plenty of food and shelter.
☐ c. are allowed to live in people's homes.
☐ d. want to become pets.   _____

Clarifying Devices   **5** The swifts' flight looks like "water swirling down a pipe." This means

☐ a. they fly straight down into the chimney.
☐ b. they fly in circles as they get closer and closer to the chimney.
☐ c. they drop into the chimney quickly.
☐ d. they fly into the chimney all at once.   _____

Vocabulary in Context   **6** When a bird hovers it

☐ a. perches.
☐ b. stays in one place in the air.
☐ c. flies in circles.
☐ d. flutters about.   _____

Add your scores for questions 1-6. Enter the total here and on the graph on page 235.

Total Score ☐

13

Life Near the North Pole

Imagine going to sleep in October and waking up in May! Well, marmots and ground squirrels stay warm by sleeping all winter. All this time, they do not wake up once. This special kind of sleep is called hibernation. During this sleep, the heart slows down, and the animal breathes more slowly. It doesn't move around, so it uses less energy.

Animals like the marmot and the ground squirrel <u>inhabit</u> the coldest parts of the world. They need special talents to survive in these frigid places. Their furry coats keep them snug when the temperature falls below zero. It often gets this cold in the Arctic, a land that is just below the North Pole.

Before the long winter, some animals eat and eat. After a while, they grow very fat. When the winter comes, they live on the fat saved up in their bodies. Layers of fat help keep an animal warm.

Arctic animals also have other ways to beat the cold. Rabbits in the Arctic, for example, have very small ears. Small ears keep heat in, while big ears let it out. Small things usually keep heat in. Have you ever slept in a room that is very small, and noticed how hot it can get?

It rarely gets warm in the Arctic. But although summer seasons there are very short, the sun shines brightly. Plants seem to spring up before your eyes! Animals such as caribou look forward all year to summer, when they can eat fresh grass again. Every minute of sunshine is important to their lives.

Main Idea	1		Answer	Score
		Mark the *main idea* →	M	15
		Mark the statement that is *too broad* →	B	5
		Mark the statement that is *too narrow* →	N	5

a. Some animals live in cold parts of the globe. ☐ _____

b. Arctic animals have many ways of keeping out the cold. ☐ _____

c. Some Arctic animals hibernate. ☐ _____

Score 15 points for each correct answer.

Subject Matter   **2**   Another good title for this passage would be

☐ a. The Arctic Summer.
☐ b. Marmots and Squirrels.
☐ c. Keeping Warm in the Arctic.
☐ d. Freezing Temperatures.

_____

Supporting Details   **3**   The Arctic is a land

☐ a. near the equator.
☐ b. near the South Pole.
☐ c. without any sunlight.
☐ d. just below the North Pole.

_____

Conclusion   **4**   After reading this passage, we can guess that when an animal moves around, it

☐ a. is very restless.
☐ b. uses more energy.
☐ c. is looking for food.
☐ d. has lost its young.

_____

Clarifying Devices   **5**   To help the reader understand that small things keep heat in, the writer uses

☐ a. an example.
☐ b. a strong argument.
☐ c. scientific facts.
☐ d. careful measurements.

_____

Vocabulary in Context   **6**   <u>Inhabit</u> means

☐ a. roam.
☐ b. survive.
☐ c. live in.
☐ d. fear.

_____

Add your scores for questions 1-6. Enter the total here and on the graph on page 235.

Total Score ☐

14

Outsmarting the Enemy

When a garden warbler sings from trees or bushes, no one can see it. The colors of this songbird match the colors of the leaves. When an animal blends in with its surroundings, its enemies can't see it either. This kind of protection is called camouflage.

Birds must protect themselves from their enemies. Sometimes this means having to fight. Sometimes it means fooling the enemy. Sometimes it means being able to escape. Birds must also protect their eggs and their young. Cats, rats and foxes love eggs for breakfast! They prowl around looking for eggs and young chicks to eat. How can birds defend themselves against such enemies?

Each species has its own way of defending itself. Birds called common terns fight with their beaks and claws. In a swarm, they peck and scratch at anyone who comes too close to their nests. Ostriches protect themselves by escaping. They can't fly, but they can run very fast. They have long, muscular legs. Ostriches can reach speeds of up to forty miles per hour. How fast is this? Well, if the wind blows this hard, it can rip huge branches from trees.

A bird called the killdeer has a lot of courage. It cares very much for its young. It would rather die than see its eggs eaten by a fox. If a fox wanders toward the nest, the killdeer pretends to be hurt. Dragging one wing, it hops away from the nest and draws the hungry fox after it.

Main Idea	1		Answer	Score
		Mark the *main idea* ⟶	M	15
		Mark the statement that is *too broad* ⟶	B	5
		Mark the statement that is *too narrow* ⟶	N	5
		a. All birds try to avoid their enemies.	☐	___
		b. Birds have many ways of defending themselves.	☐	___
		c. The ostrich defends itself best by running fast.	☐	___

Score 15 points for each correct answer.   **Score**

Subject Matter **2** This passage is concerned with
- ☐ a. songbirds.
- ☐ b. foxes.
- ☐ c. bird defense.
- ☐ d. hiding.

_____

Supporting Details **3** The killdeer tricks the fox by
- ☐ a. feeding him eggs.
- ☐ b. pretending to be hurt.
- ☐ c. flying away.
- ☐ d. changing color.

_____

Conclusion **4** We can conclude from this passage that the killdeer
- ☐ a. wants its babies to survive.
- ☐ b. gets hurt easily.
- ☐ c. hops on one leg.
- ☐ d. pretends to like foxes.

_____

Clarifying Devices **5** "If the wind blows this hard, it can rip huge branches from the trees" refers to the ostrich's
- ☐ a. strength.
- ☐ b. temper.
- ☐ c. speed.
- ☐ d. power.

_____

Vocabulary in Context **6** A swarm is a
- ☐ a. cluster.
- ☐ b. nest.
- ☐ c. tree.
- ☐ d. frenzy.

_____

Add your scores for questions 1-6. Enter the total here and on the graph on page 235.

Total Score ☐

15

The Largest Walking Animal

What is the biggest land animal on earth? If you guessed the elephant, you are absolutely right. An elephant can be almost twice as tall as a pony. It can weigh as much as a small truck.

Because they are <u>enormous</u>, elephants are very strong. Like cranes or tractors, elephants can do jobs that are too difficult for people. Their trunks are one of their most useful tools. With its trunk, an elephant can lift a telephone pole! The trunk can also be used for small jobs, like munching grass or gathering peanuts.

Long, white tusks grow on either side of the trunk. The tusks can grow to be eight feet long. Elephants use their tusks for fighting and for picking things up. Often, the right tusk is shorter than the left tusk. This is because the elephant uses it more. With use, the tusk wears down like a pencil that has been used for years of writing.

The bony tusks are made of ivory. Since times long past, men have hunted elephants for their ivory. Because so many people want it, ivory has always been thought precious. It is used for making carvings, jewelry and piano keys. But the killing of elephants for ivory has endangered the whole species. As time goes on, there are fewer and fewer elephants. If the killing keeps up, there may be none left at all! And who can imagine a world without its largest walking animal?

Main Idea	1		Answer	Score
	Mark the *main idea* ⟶	M		15
	Mark the statement that is *too broad* ⟶	B		5
	Mark the statement that is *too narrow* ⟶	N		5
	a. Elephants are very strong.	☐		___
	b. There are many different kinds of animals in the world.	☐		___
	c. Elephants are the biggest land animals on earth.	☐		___

Score 15 points for each correct answer.

Subject Matter

2 This passage is mainly about
- ☐ a. strong animals.
- ☐ b. tools.
- ☐ c. elephants.
- ☐ d. ivory.

_____

Supporting Details

3 An elephant gathers peanuts with its
- ☐ a. tusks.
- ☐ b. trunk.
- ☐ c. mouth.
- ☐ d. ivory.

_____

Conclusion

4 The author of this passage feels that
- ☐ a. elephants cannot protect themselves.
- ☐ b. elephants should be hunted for ivory.
- ☐ c. ivory is very important.
- ☐ d. elephants should not be hunted for ivory.

_____

Clarifying Devices

5 The first sentence creates interest by
- ☐ a. making a strong statement.
- ☐ b. asking a question.
- ☐ c. using a comparison.
- ☐ d. making an analogy.

_____

Vocabulary in Context

6 By <u>enormous</u>, the writer means that the elephant is
- ☐ a. very strong.
- ☐ b. intelligent.
- ☐ c. very big.
- ☐ d. slow moving.

_____

Add your scores for questions 1-6. Enter the total here and on the graph on page 235.

Total Score ☐

53

16

Put a Lid on It

Sports have always been ruled by the weather. Rain, sleet, snow and cold called the plays. Baseball fans have often sat in the rain without cover, waiting for the sun to come out and the game to begin. Football lovers sometimes took days to warm up after sitting through a freezing cold Sunday game. For both sports fans and players, the domed stadium was like something out of a dream. A huge plastic bubble kept out rain and snow. There was heat to keep things comfortable year round.

Domed stadiums have clearly changed the <u>course</u> of sports. Still, they did have their problems at first. Most of these problems were discovered and solved at the Houston Astrodome. This was the world's first stadium with a lid. For the fans, it was great. But there were some problems for the players. Baseball outfielders had the most difficult time. They had to learn to catch in a field with a roof. At first this was almost as difficult as playing in the dark. The panes of the roof were light colored, to let sunlight in. Sunlight was needed to keep the grass on the field alive. But the light roof blended too well with the white baseball. Fly balls seemed to drop out of nowhere. Even skilled fielders were making errors. Finally, the decision was made to paint the panes of the roof dark. The problem was solved. But what about the grass? Well, the real grass was dug up and replaced with artificial turf!

Main Idea	1		Answer	Score
	Mark the *main idea* ⟶		**M**	15
	Mark the statement that is *too broad* ⟶		**B**	5
	Mark the statement that is *too narrow* ⟶		**N**	5

a. Over the years there have been improvements that have made watching sports more comfortable. ☐ ____

b. The domed stadium made it possible for sports to be played in any weather. ☐ ____

c. Sports have always depended on the weather. ☐ ____

Subject Matter **2** This passage is about
- ☐ a. baseball games.
- ☐ b. cold weather.
- ☐ c. how to play outfield.
- ☐ d. domed stadiums.

Supporting Details **3** Domed stadiums must have
- ☐ a. artificial grass.
- ☐ b. bright sunlight.
- ☐ c. stained glass roofs.
- ☐ d. bright lighting.

Conclusion **4** We can conclude that domed stadiums are
- ☐ a. a thing of the past.
- ☐ b. a passing fad.
- ☐ c. revolutionizing sports.
- ☐ d. expensive to keep up.

Clarifying Devices **5** Hyperbole is a literary device which is an exaggerated statement. Choose the hyperbole from the examples below.
- ☐ a. Sports have always been ruled by the weather.
- ☐ b. Football lovers sometimes took days to warm up after a freezing cold Sunday game.
- ☐ c. It was the world's first stadium with a lid.
- ☐ d. At first this was almost as difficult as playing in the dark.

Vocabulary in Context **6** In this passage the word <u>course</u> means
- ☐ a. a place for a race.
- ☐ b. a school of study.
- ☐ c. the direction.
- ☐ d. part of a meal.

Add your scores for questions 1-6. Enter the total here and on the graph on page 235.   Total Score ☐

17

Thanks to Friendly Insects

Would you like an insect for a friend? Well, many insects are very friendly and useful to human beings. The lac insect of India, for instance, is prized by many people. It oozes a sticky liquid from which shellac is made. Shellac is used to varnish wood. Some insects are used to make food coloring. The cochineal insect has a substance that is used to make red dye.

Some insects help us grow food. They eat plants and bugs that harm crops. The cactus moth once saved miles of pasture land in this way. In Australia, the prickly pear cactus was destroying pastures one by one. Like a "giant blob" in a science fiction movie, it grew everywhere. It choked small plants. Thousands of cactus moths were shipped to Australia to help. The moths went to work. They <u>devoured</u> the prickly pear cactus.

Without insects, we would have a hard time growing plants. Butterflies and bees help the fruit to grow. They serve a very important purpose. They carry pollen from flower to flower in the apple trees. Pollen must be carried between flowers for the trees to make seeds. Without seeds, there would be no fruit. Thanks insects!

Main Idea	1		Answer	Score
		Mark the *main idea* ⟶	M	15
		Mark the statement that is *too broad* ⟶	B	5
		Mark the statement that is *too narrow* ⟶	N	5

a. Butterflies and bees are helpful to human beings. ☐ _____

b. Many insects are helpful to human beings. ☐ _____

c. Insects are interesting creatures. ☐ _____

Score 15 points for each correct answer.

Subject Matter

2 This passage is about insects that are
- ☐ a. friends of people.
- ☐ b. enemies of people.
- ☐ c. useful in Australia.
- ☐ d. friends of flowers.

_____

Supporting Details

3 The cochineal insect gives us
- ☐ a. shellac.
- ☐ b. red dye.
- ☐ c. pollen.
- ☐ d. food coloring.

_____

Conclusion

4 Wherever the cactus moth lives, you would <u>not</u> expect to find
- ☐ a. pastures of grass.
- ☐ b. a hot climate.
- ☐ c. other insects.
- ☐ d. the prickly pear cactus.

_____

Clarifying Devices

5 The author's main purpose in writing this passage is to
- ☐ a. give you information.
- ☐ b. make you laugh.
- ☐ c. frighten you.
- ☐ d. convince you.

_____

Vocabulary in Context

6 In this passage, the word <u>devoured</u> means
- ☐ a. ate greedily.
- ☐ b. cut into pieces.
- ☐ c. gathered quickly.
- ☐ d. ignored.

_____

Add your scores for questions 1–6. Enter the total here and on the graph on page 235.

Total Score ☐

18

Feathery Homes

Did you know that there is a kind of bird that can sew? It is called the tailorbird. It uses its beak as a needle. It sews leaves together in the shape of a cup. Then it lines the cup with straw and lays its eggs there.

Each species builds its own special kind of nest. The most common materials used for nests are grasses, twigs and feathers. A bird must weave these materials into a nest. Imagine building a house without cement or nails to hold it together!

A weaverbird builds a nest that looks like a basket. It is shaped like a pear with a hole in the middle. The hole is the door of the nest.

The ovenbird makes a nest that is very solid. The nest is made of mud. Like a sculptor, the ovenbird <u>molds</u> the mud into the shape of an oven and then lets it dry in the sun. The sun bakes the mud, making it very hard.

Not all birds make their homes in branches. Some birds build their nests on the ground. Others bury their eggs under the ground. Some birds do not build nests at all. For example, a bird called the fairy tern lays its eggs right on a branch. It tiptoes on the branch and balances its eggs very carefully so they won't fall. So, when you look for nests and eggs in the branches of trees and bushes, remember that some nests may be right under your feet!

Main Idea   1

	Answer	Score
Mark the *main idea* ⟶	M	15
Mark the statement that is *too broad* ⟶	B	5
Mark the statement that is *too narrow* ⟶	N	5

a. Some birds build their nests on the ground. ☐ _____

b. Each type of bird builds a special kind of nest. ☐ _____

c. There are many species of birds. ☐ _____

Score 15 points for each correct answer.   **Score**

Subject Matter

2 This passage centers on
- [ ] a. the many kinds of birds.
- [ ] b. the building of bird nests.
- [ ] c. the ovenbird.
- [ ] d. unusual birds.

Supporting Details

3 The ovenbird builds its nest of
- [ ] a. straw.
- [ ] b. grass.
- [ ] c. mud.
- [ ] d. twigs.

Conclusion

4 The writer of this passage admires
- [ ] a. the bright colors of the tailorbird.
- [ ] b. birds that bury their eggs.
- [ ] c. the basket-shaped nest of the weaverbird.
- [ ] d. the effort it takes to build a nest.

Clarifying Devices

5 The writer compares the ovenbird to a
- [ ] a. tailor.
- [ ] b. sculptor.
- [ ] c. weaver.
- [ ] d. carpenter.

Vocabulary in Context

6 The word molds means
- [ ] a. weaves.
- [ ] b. shapes.
- [ ] c. pours.
- [ ] d. gathers.

Add your scores for questions 1-6. Enter the total here and on the graph on page 235.

Total Score

19

Give Them a Hand

Right is right. Right? Of course. But is left wrong? Well, the ancient Romans thought so. As far as they were concerned, left-handed people were mistakes of nature. Latin, the language of the Romans, had many words that expressed this view. Some words we use today still have this meaning. The Latin word *dexter* means "right." The English word *dexterous* comes from this word. It means "handy." So, right is handy. But the Latin word for left is *sinistra*. The English word *sinister* was derived from this word. Sinister means "evil." Is it fair to call righties handy and lefties evil? Well, fair or not, many languages have words that express similar beliefs. In Old English, the word for left means "weak." That isn't much of an improvement over "evil."

Not very long ago, <u>southpaws</u> were often forced to write with their right hands. Doctors have since found that this can be very harmful. You should use the hand you were born to use.

People who use their left hands are just starting to get better treatment. But why all the name calling in the first place? One reason may be that there are not as many left-handed people as there are right-handed people. There is one lefty for every five righties. People who are different are often thought to be wrong. But attitudes do seem to be changing. Fair-minded right-handed people are finally starting to give lefties a hand.

Main Idea	1			Answer	Score
		Mark the *main idea* —→		M	15
		Mark the statement that is *too broad* —→		B	5
		Mark the statement that is *too narrow* —→		N	5

a. Many languages have words that express the idea that left is bad. ☐ _____

b. Minorities often get bad treatment. ☐ _____

c. Throughout history, left-handed people have been treated poorly. ☐ _____

Subject Matter

2 This passage is about

☐ a. Latin words.

☐ b. the ancient Romans.

☐ c. attitudes toward left-handed people.

☐ d. weak and evil people. _____

Supporting Details

3 At one time, people who were left-handed were

☐ a. laughed at.

☐ b. very clumsy.

☐ c. forced to use their right hands.

☐ d. admired. _____

Conclusion

4 Lefties today are

☐ a. just as weak as lefties of the past.

☐ b. being treated better than lefties of the past.

☐ c. thought to be strange.

☐ d. being taught to use their right hands. _____

Clarifying Devices

5 "Fair-minded right-handed people are finally starting to give lefties a hand" means that they are

☐ a. applauding them.

☐ b. teaching them how to use their right hands.

☐ c. starting to give them a chance and help them out.

☐ d. shaking hands with them. _____

Vocabulary in Context

6 A <u>southpaw</u> is

☐ a. a type of bear.

☐ b. a Roman citizen.

☐ c. a left-handed person.

☐ d. a person from the South. _____

Add your scores for questions 1-6. Enter the total here and on the graph on page 235.   **Total Score** ☐

61

20

A Perfect Match

One man's search for gold ended in a book of matches. The first matches were made by a German alchemist. Like others of his time, he was trying to make gold. But instead, he came up with phosphorous. This chemical is so sensitive that it bursts into flame when exposed to the air. The first match was made in 1680. In those days few people could afford even an ounce of phosphorous. It was so expensive that lighting a match was like burning money. The first matches were toys for the rich. They were not matches as we know them. They were small bottles containing pieces of paper dipped in phosphorous. When exposed to the air, they caught fire.

It was not until 1827, in England, that the type of match we are familiar with was made. It used phosphorous too, but in smaller amounts. It was lighted by friction. Everyone could afford these matches. They replaced flint and steel, which for ages had been the only tools for starting fires. But these matches proved to be a curse as well as a blessing. Phosphorous is a deadly poison. The people who made matches often died from a disease caused by the poison. Babies died from swallowing match heads. Some people used them to commit suicide.

At last, in 1911, William Fairburn devised a <u>nontoxic</u> type of phosphorous. He proved himself an unselfish man by giving the formula to all the match makers, rather than keeping it for his own profit.

Main Idea	1		Answer	Score
		Mark the *main idea* →	M	15
		Mark the statement that is *too broad* →	B	5
		Mark the statement that is *too narrow* →	N	5

a. Matches went through many stages of development before the modern match was invented. ☐ _____

b. The phosphorous used in early matches was deadly poisonous. ☐ _____

c. Matches are made from chemicals. ☐ _____

Subject Matter

2 This passage deals with

☐ a. the dangers of phosphorous.

☐ b. the invention of gold.

☐ c. the invention of matches.

☐ d. flint and steel.

_____

Supporting Details

3 Phosphorous was a good chemical to use for matches because it was very

☐ a. poisonous.

☐ b. expensive.

☐ c. flammable.

☐ d. fire resistant.

_____

Conclusion

4 Fairburn's decision to share his formula probably caused him to lose

☐ a. bets.

☐ b. friends.

☐ c. money.

☐ d. respect.

_____

Clarifying Devices

5 The author compares lighting one of the earliest matches to burning money in order to describe

☐ a. how unlikely it was that an inexpensive match could be made.

☐ b. how foolishly people spent their money.

☐ c. how expensive phosphorous was.

☐ d. how flammable phosphorous was.

_____

Vocabulary in Context

6 Nontoxic means

☐ a. unsafe.

☐ b. not poisonous.

☐ c. inexpensive.

☐ d. less flammable.

_____

Add your scores for questions 1-6. Enter the total here and on the graph on page 235.

Total Score ☐

21

The Hermit

Most people like living with other people. But, some people just have to be by themselves. Take Bozo Kucik, for example. For over 84 years Bozo lived all alone on a desert island.

In 1888, when Bozo was only 16, his father left him on a little island off the coast of Yugoslavia. He kissed Bozo goodbye and said, "I hope all goes well with you, my son." Then the father got back in his boat and sailed home without his son. How could he do such a thing, you ask? Well, Bozo had asked him to.

Bozo's father was a poor peasant who couldn't afford to feed his seven children. So he called his sons together and asked them to decide their own futures. Bozo chose the life of a hermit.

During the years that Bozo lived alone, World Wars I and II were fought. But Bozo never heard about them. In 1972, a crew of fishermen visited his island. They tried to talk to Bozo. At first the old hermit ran away. Finally, he let the men into his windowless stone hut.

The fishermen talked with Bozo for over two hours. They told him all about the two world wars he had missed. When they asked his age, Bozo said he guessed he was 100 years old.

They asked if he wanted to go home, but Bozo said no. So the fishermen wished Bozo well and left him alone again—just as his father had 84 years before.

Main Idea	1		Answer	Score
	Mark the *main idea* ⟶	M		15
	Mark the statement that is *too broad* ⟶	B		5
	Mark the statement that is *too narrow* ⟶	N		5

a. Bozo lived alone on an island for 84 years. ☐ _____

b. Bozo's father left him on a desert island. ☐ _____

c. Many people wish to live alone. ☐ _____

Subject Matter **2** Another good title for the passage would be

☐ a. Living Alone.
☐ b. 84 Years Alone.
☐ c. Why Bozo Left Home.
☐ d. A Desert Island.   _____

Supporting Details **3** According to the passage, Bozo's father was a

☐ a. fisherman.
☐ b. hermit.
☐ c. peasant.
☐ d. soldier.   _____

Conclusion **4** One can assume from the passage that Bozo <u>definitely did not have</u> which of the following?

☐ a. Tools
☐ b. Clothes
☐ c. Radio
☐ d. Food   _____

Clarifying Devices **5** When Bozo first saw the fishermen he was

☐ a. frightened.
☐ b. overjoyed.
☐ c. curious.
☐ d. angry.   _____

Vocabulary in Context **6** The best definition for the word <u>hermit</u> is someone who

☐ a. doesn't like people.
☐ b. lives on an island.
☐ c. lives alone.
☐ d. likes quiet.   _____

Add your scores for questions 1-6. Enter the total here and on the graph on page 236.   **Total Score** ☐

22

They'll Eat Anything

You know that pearls grow inside oysters, but would you ever think to look for diamonds inside an ostrich? Well, a hunter once shot an ostrich and discovered, to his great surprise, that the big bird had swallowed a bunch of diamonds. How could such a strange thing happen?

Like many other birds, the ostrich swallows small stones that stay inside its "gizzard." The gizzard is a bird's second stomach. It is where the food is ground up. The small stones help to grind up the food so it can be digested. They do the chewing, because birds don't have teeth. In the case of the ostrich with the diamonds, the bird simply had expensive taste in rocks. He used the diamonds to help digest his dinner.

Diamonds and stones aren't all that an ostrich will swallow. If there are no stones around, it will eat just about anything. Sadly for ostriches in zoos this can be a <u>fatal</u> habit. The tendency to swallow anything it sees has caused the death of many an ostrich. Cruel or careless people often throw things into the bird's living space. They throw keys, coins, even large objects such as horseshoes. The ostrich swallows them without hesitation. Coins can be the worst. Inside the ostrich they wear down to a razor sharp edge. They will cut open the bird's gizzard from the inside. One young zoo ostrich died with 484 coins, weighing more than eight pounds, in its gizzard.

Main Idea	1		Answer	Score
		Mark the *main idea* ⟶	M	15
		Mark the statement that is *too broad* ⟶	B	5
		Mark the statement that is *too narrow* ⟶	N	5
		a. Birds often eat strange things.	☐	____
		b. Ostriches will swallow anything to help them digest food, if stones are not available.	☐	____
		c. Stones are important to the ostrich's digestion.	☐	____

Score 15 points for each correct answer.   **Score**

Subject Matter **2** This passage is about
- ☐ a. ostriches.
- ☐ b. diamonds.
- ☐ c. people at the zoo.
- ☐ d. rock hunting.

_____

Supporting Details **3** Ostriches eat stones because they don't have
- ☐ a. enough food.
- ☐ b. bird seed.
- ☐ c. teeth.
- ☐ d. diamonds.

_____

Conclusion **4** The ostrich is not smart enough to
- ☐ a. digest its own food.
- ☐ b. eat only diamonds.
- ☐ c. avoid eating objects that are harmful.
- ☐ d. escape from the zoo.

_____

Clarifying Devices **5** The phrase "They do the chewing" makes the rocks seem as though they are
- ☐ a. important.
- ☐ b. alive.
- ☐ c. dangerous.
- ☐ d. uncomfortable.

_____

Vocabulary in Context **6** Fatal is another word for
- ☐ a. foolish.
- ☐ b. careless.
- ☐ c. deadly.
- ☐ d. cruel.

_____

Add your scores for questions 1-6. Enter the total here and on the graph on page 236.

Total Score ☐

23

Isis Plays

Have you ever seen an old movie in which the villain was a robot? Such movies were made when robots were thought of as mechanical monsters that could control people. This, of course, all came from the minds of science fiction writers. Still, thanks to these films, a lot of people think robots are just evil. These people have never met Isis.

In 1940, a man named Cecil Nixon invented a robot named Isis. He made his robot in the <u>form</u> of a beautiful woman. She was named after the chief goddess of ancient Egypt. Nixon's Isis could play a musical instrument called a zither. A zither is a small stringed instrument that is plucked and strummed like a harp. Isis would rest on a couch with a zither in her lap. She could play 3,000 different tunes on the zither. All you had to do was ask her to play. Dr. Nixon had made her in such a way that she would respond to the human voice. Isis played the instrument with her hands. Dr. Nixon also made Isis react to heat. When it got too warm she would lift a veil from her face. Isis's movements were controlled by thousands of wheels and hundreds of magnets. Electronic robots were still a thing of the future. Although Isis was just a machine, sometimes she seemed almost human.

Main Idea 1

	Answer	Score
Mark the *main idea* ⟶	M	15
Mark the statement that is *too broad* ⟶	B	5
Mark the statement that is *too narrow* ⟶	N	5

a. Isis was a mechanical robot that could play songs on a zither. ☐ ____

b. Robots can do many amazing things. ☐ ____

c. Isis reacted to the sound of people's voices. ☐ ____

Score 15 points for each correct answer.   **Score**

Subject Matter

2 This passage is about
- ☐ a. evil robots.
- ☐ b. a robot that could play a zither.
- ☐ c. Dr. Nixon's many projects.
- ☐ d. robots in the movies.   _____

Supporting Details

3 The secret to Isis is
- ☐ a. a real woman who hides inside her.
- ☐ b. her magic veil.
- ☐ c. a computer.
- ☐ d. thousands of wheels and hundreds of magnets.   _____

Conclusion

4 We can conclude that Isis was
- ☐ a. destroyed by fire.
- ☐ b. not very lifelike.
- ☐ c. built before the days of transistors and integrated circuits.
- ☐ d. used in old movies.   _____

Clarifying Devices

5 The writer makes a comparison between early robots in movies and Isis in order to
- ☐ a. show us that robots can be good and beautiful.
- ☐ b. show us that science fiction writers were liars.
- ☐ c. show us that robots cannot be evil.
- ☐ d. make us hate old movies.   _____

Vocabulary in Context

6 In this passage <u>form</u> means
- ☐ a. mold.
- ☐ b. manner.
- ☐ c. home.
- ☐ d. appearance.   _____

Add your scores for questions 1-6. Enter the total here and on the graph on page 236.

Total Score ☐

24

Confused Whales

In June of 1973, nine whales beached on the Florida coast. Beaching means swimming out of the ocean onto the beach, and usually dying there. No one knows why they do it, but a number of whales beach themselves every year. Some people think beaching is an accident.

Perhaps the whales get confused. Scientists who studied the beaching of three dozen whales in Australia think the whales may have been confused by loud noises. Whales can tell where they are by sounds. They send out sounds and listen as they travel past or bounce off objects. Two days before these thirty-six whales beached, loud guns had been fired for two hours. The loud sounds may have confused the whales. Their confusion might have caused them to <u>wander</u> into low water.

Whatever the reason whales beach, it is a sad event. People try to save them, but very few beached whales live. One whale that was rescued from beaching in Florida lived for forty-five days. That is the longest a beached whale has ever survived. And it lived that long only because it got attention from doctors.

All over the world, scientists rush to whale beachings as soon as they hear about them. They hope to learn why whales beach, and how to save them.

Main Idea	1		Answer	Score
		Mark the *main idea* ⟶	M	15
		Mark the statement that is *too broad* ⟶	B	5
		Mark the statement that is *too narrow* ⟶	N	5

a. The longest a beached whale has lived is forty-five days. ☐ _____

b. Each year whales beach themselves, and no one knows why. ☐ _____

c. Sea animals often die by beaching themselves. ☐ _____

Score 15 points for each correct answer.

Subject Matter

2 The subject of this passage is

☐ a. the Florida beaches.

☐ b. beached whales.

☐ c. whale sounds.

☐ d. medical treatment of whales.

_____

Supporting Details

3 One reason whales beach may be

☐ a. because they are hungry.

☐ b. because they are attacked.

☐ c. so that people can study them.

☐ d. that they are confused.

_____

Conclusion

4 Whale beachings are sad events because

☐ a. people know the whales are going to die.

☐ b. the whales have to be carted away and buried.

☐ c. the whales cannot be used as food.

☐ d. no one can use the beach on those days.

_____

Clarifying Devices

5 To make the point that beached whales do not survive, the author uses

☐ a. the opinions of famous people.

☐ b. a vivid word picture.

☐ c. an example.

☐ d. a firsthand story.

_____

Vocabulary in Context

6 In this passage, <u>wander</u> means

☐ a. rush.

☐ b. roam.

☐ c. forget.

☐ d. swim.

_____

Add your scores for questions 1-6. Enter the total here and on the graph on page 236.

Total Score ☐

25

Forever Amber

Amber lasts and lasts. Scientists are very glad of this. Without amber, we would not have many of the world's most important fossils. Amber is a hard, yellowish-brown resin found in the earth. It is translucent, which means you can see through it. It is known for its ability to preserve things.

Long ago, amber was not as hard as it is today. It was soft and gummy. Insects that weren't careful about where they walked often got trapped in it. The poor bugs that got caught in the sticky amber died. But they were forever preserved. The golden resin worked like a wax mold. It shaped itself around the insects. The resin hardened as the bodies of the dead insects slowly decayed. The last traces of the insects trapped in amber have been gone for thousands of years. But the imprints of their bodies remained fixed in the hardened resin. Although the bugs are gone from the earth, their imprints remain for us to study. Many of these imprints are very fine and detailed. Preserved imprints of creatures and plants that once lived are called fossils. They help scientists learn more about life on earth in the past.

Main Idea	1		Answer	Score
		Mark the *main idea* ⟶	M	15
		Mark the statement that is *too broad* ⟶	B	5
		Mark the statement that is *too narrow* ⟶	N	5

a. Objects from long ago can tell us a lot about our past. ☐ _____

b. Amber has preserved the shapes of ancient creatures. ☐ _____

c. Amber is a hard resin that preserved things. ☐ _____

Score 15 points for each correct answer.

Subject Matter **2** This passage is about

    ☐ a. the properties of amber.

    ☐ b. how amber preserved things.

    ☐ c. how amber resin hardened.

    ☐ d. how amber was found.

Supporting Details **3** Insects that walked in amber

    ☐ a. got stuck in the gooey substance.

    ☐ b. found it to be slippery.

    ☐ c. used it to build their nests.

    ☐ d. became very hard.

Conclusion **4** We can conclude from this passage that amber

    ☐ a. has almost disappeared from the earth.

    ☐ b. is produced by dead insects.

    ☐ c. has played an important role in the study of prehistoric creatures.

    ☐ d. is used to make candles.

Clarifying Devices **5** The gummy amber resin acted like

    ☐ a. glue.

    ☐ b. a dead insect.

    ☐ c. a wax mold.

    ☐ d. a fossil.

Vocabulary in Context **6** In this case <u>mold</u> means

    ☐ a. a fungus.

    ☐ b. a form used to make a special shape.

    ☐ c. rich earth.

    ☐ d. to influence.

Add your scores for questions 1-6. Enter the total here and on the graph on page 236.

Total Score ☐

26

Jumbo

Jumbo the elephant is one of the most famous animals that ever lived. He was the biggest elephant and the proudest possession of the British Crown.

In April of 1882, he was shipped to a zoo in the United States for a visit. He was an instant success. P.T. Barnum had heard of this giant and the great crowds he attracted. Barnum decided that he would like to have Jumbo in his circus. He thought of a way to get him. Barnum knew that elephants in captivity have <u>periodic</u> fits of violence. He waited for Jumbo to have such a fit. When it happened, he asked the zoo to sell him the elephant. Jumbo was sold to Barnum, who paid on the spot. He became the star of the circus. Barnum made a fortune on this star.

But one day tragedy struck Jumbo. It was after a show. The elephant was being led back to his cage near the railroad tracks by his trainers. Suddenly, a bright light blinded them. A train whistled, and brakes screeched as the engineer tried to stop. Dazzled by the light, Jumbo charged right into it. There was a crash that chilled the hearts of those who were there. The confused animal had run head-on into the train's engine. Jumbo died of a broken neck.

Main Idea	1		Answer	Score
		Mark the *main idea* →	M	15
		Mark the statement that is *too broad* →	B	5
		Mark the statement that is *too narrow* →	N	5

a. Jumbo, the world's most famous circus elephant, was killed by a train. ☐ _____

b. Jumbo's circus career ended in tragedy. ☐ _____

c. Elephants are great circus attractions. ☐ _____

Score 15 points for each correct answer.

Subject Matter

2 Another good title for this passage would be
- ☐ a. Under the Big Top.
- ☐ b. P.T. Barnum's Circus.
- ☐ c. The Train That Killed Jumbo.
- ☐ d. The World's Most Famous Elephant.   _____

Supporting Details

3 P.T. Barnum
- ☐ a. was the head of a British zoo.
- ☐ b. killed Jumbo.
- ☐ c. stole Jumbo from the British.
- ☐ d. bought Jumbo for his circus.   _____

Conclusion

4 Which of the following is most likely true?
- ☐ a. Jumbo was the biggest elephant known.
- ☐ b. Jumbo probably didn't die immediately after the crash.
- ☐ c. Jumbo could have been saved by surgery.
- ☐ d. Jumbo may have wanted to end his own life when he charged into the train.   _____

Clarifying Devices

5 The phrase "chilled the hearts of those who were there" means that those who saw Jumbo killed
- ☐ a. had no feelings.
- ☐ b. were fascinated.
- ☐ c. were shocked and upset.
- ☐ d. hated Jumbo.   _____

Vocabulary in Context

6 A "periodic fit of violence" is one that
- ☐ a. occurs every once in a while.
- ☐ b. happens only once.
- ☐ c. results in someone's death.
- ☐ d. is very surprising.   _____

Add your scores for questions 1-6. Enter the total here and on the graph on page 236.   Total Score [ ]

75

27

Slow but Sure

Today, the Indianapolis 500, one of the world's most famous car races, takes about four hours to run. If the Indy 500 had been held in 1895, it would have taken almost three days. The horseless carriage had just been invented a short time before. Top speeds back then were much lower than they are today. For most people, just seeing a car move without a horse pulling it was thrilling enough. The driver's main concern was making sure the car didn't break down.

One of the first car races was held in Chicago on Thanksgiving Day in 1895. Folks crowded the streets to <u>gawk</u> at the new machines. The route of the race went through the heart of town. The cars were to go out to a nearby suburb and back. The race covered a distance of about 54 miles. That's less than one-tenth the distance at Indy. The drivers cranked up their engines and prayed that they wouldn't konk out. Then they were off. The race proved too much for some of the cars. Perhaps they couldn't withstand the high speeds. The winner of the contest was J. Frank Duryea. He got the checkered flag a bit more than seven hours after he started. He had covered the grueling distance at an average speed of 7.5 miles per hour. That is slower than a modern marathoner can go on foot. Even so, as Duryea finished, the crowd went wild.

Main Idea   1

	Answer	Score
Mark the *main idea* ⟶	M	15
Mark the statement that is *too broad* ⟶	B	5
Mark the statement that is *too narrow* ⟶	N	5

a. Things don't have to be done quickly to be done well. ☐ _____

b. Early auto races were very slow compared with today's races. ☐ _____

c. The first autos could not go very fast. ☐ _____

Score 15 points for each correct answer.   **Score**

Subject Matter

2 This passage deals with
- ☐ a. the Indianapolis 500.
- ☐ b. a new kind of car.
- ☐ c. an early auto race.
- ☐ d. the streets of Chicago.   _____

Supporting Details

3 Some cars didn't finish the race in Chicago because
- ☐ a. their engines broke down.
- ☐ b. the drivers were afraid of the high speeds.
- ☐ c. the brakes jammed.
- ☐ d. they ran out of gas.   _____

Conclusion

4 What can you conclude about the public's attitude toward auto races?
- ☐ a. They were more impressed with slower speeds.
- ☐ b. They thought cars were unnecessary.
- ☐ c. They enjoyed just seeing the cars.
- ☐ d. They were easily bored.   _____

Clarifying Devices

5 This passage is mainly
- ☐ a. a description of an event.
- ☐ b. a set of historical facts.
- ☐ c. a list of racing statistics.
- ☐ d. the biography of an auto racer.   _____

Vocabulary in Context

6 In this passage the word <u>gawk</u> means
- ☐ a. laugh.
- ☐ b. stare.
- ☐ c. frown.
- ☐ d. glare.   _____

Add your scores for questions 1-6. Enter the total here and on the graph on page 236.

Total Score ☐

28

The Wizard of Wall Street

At the age of eighty, Hetty Green lived like a <u>pauper</u> in an unheated apartment. To save the cost of heating her food, she ate only cold eggs and onions. In order to save more money, Hetty wore newspapers instead of underwear. She had only the bottoms of her dresses cleaned. A very poor person, you say? No, Hetty was one of America's richest women!

Hetty was born in 1835 in a rich section of Bellow Falls, Vermont. When her father died, she was left a large fortune. She took all of her money and invested it in the stock market. Her stocks did so well that she became known as "the wizard of Wall Street."

But, though she was very rich, Hetty was extremely cheap. For instance, when her son, Edward, broke his leg, she refused to call for a doctor. She felt it would cost too much. So she carried her son to a charity hospital. Still, young Edward's leg got worse. Finally, the leg had to be removed to save the boy's life. But Hetty still didn't want to pay the hospital fee. Instead, she had her son's operation done on the kitchen table in her rooming house.

When Hetty died in 1916, she was worth over one hundred and twenty million dollars. Yet, this tight-fisted woman had lived as though she barely had a cent.

Main Idea	1		Answer	Score
		Mark the *main idea* →	M	15
		Mark the statement that is *too broad* →	B	5
		Mark the statement that is *too narrow* →	N	5

a. Hetty Green was rich, but lived like a poor person. ☐ ____

b. Hetty Green didn't like to spend money. ☐ ____

c. Hetty Green was an unusual person. ☐ ____

Subject Matter

2 Another good title for this story might be

  ☐ a. How to Make a Million Dollars.
  ☐ b. The Cheap Millionaire.
  ☐ c. Poor Hetty Green.
  ☐ d. Cheap Medical Care.

Supporting Details

3 Hetty carried her son to a charity hospital because

  ☐ a. she had no money.
  ☐ b. her son refused to see a doctor.
  ☐ c. the doctor refused to come to her house.
  ☐ d. she refused to call for a doctor.

Conclusion

4 It is obvious from the passage that Hetty was

  ☐ a. very poor as a child.
  ☐ b. a very good businesswoman.
  ☐ c. afraid of doctors.
  ☐ d. poor in her old age.

Clarifying Devices

5 The author tells us about Hetty's son's accident

  ☐ a. to show us that she was a good mother.
  ☐ b. to show us how she felt about doctors.
  ☐ c. to show us how brave Edward was.
  ☐ d. to show us just how cheap she was.

Vocabulary in Context

6 What is the best definition for the word <u>pauper</u>?

  ☐ a. Greedy person
  ☐ b. Old person
  ☐ c. Poor person
  ☐ d. Cheap person

Add your scores for questions 1-6. Enter the total here and on the graph on page 236.

Total Score

29

Courage and Skill

John Paul Jones was one of the founders of the United States Navy. During the Revolution, the colonies were desperate. They needed men to lead their small ships against the British fleet. Jones was more than willing to fight.

John Paul Jones had once been a captain of a British merchant ship. In 1773, his crew mutinied. One member of the crew tried to gain control of the ship. Jones shot the man to death. The mutiny took place near the port of Tobago, an island in the Caribbean. Authorities there decided to have a trial. This meant certain death for John Paul Jones, since the whole crew would testify against him. One night during a thunderstorm, he escaped from the jail.

He fled to the United States and lived with a family named Jones. His real name was John Paul. He added the name of Jones to his, in honor of the family. He outwitted the British ships that were sent to hunt him down. And he did this with little more than his own courage and the skill of his crew.

When the American Revolution ended he went to serve in the Russian navy. There, he fought the Turks and achieved one of the few major naval victories in the history of Russia. He died in Paris at the age of forty-five.

John Paul Jones is considered both an American and Russian hero, but the English considered him a fugitive.

Main Idea	1		Answer	Score
	Mark the *main idea* ⟶		M	15
	Mark the statement that is *too broad* ⟶		B	5
	Mark the statement that is *too narrow* ⟶		N	5
	a. John Paul Jones was a skilled sailor.		☐	____
	b. John Paul Jones was a successful naval fighter.		☐	____
	c. Many brave men fought in the American Revolution.		☐	____

Score 15 points for each correct answer.   **Score**

Subject Matter

2 Another good title for this passage would be

☐ a. John Paul Jones.

☐ b. A British Merchant Seaman.

☐ c. The Greatest Naval Fighter.

☐ d. Founder of the United States Navy.   _____

Supporting Details

3 John Paul Jones won a major victory for the Russian navy against the

☐ a. French.

☐ b. British.

☐ c. Turks.

☐ d. Spanish.   _____

Conclusion

4 You can conclude from this passage that Jones was

☐ a. thoughtful.

☐ b. fearful.

☐ c. kind.

☐ d. courageous.   _____

Clarifying Devices

5 The passage is basically a

☐ a. biography of John Paul Jones.

☐ b. criticism of John Paul Jones.

☐ c. history of the United States Navy.

☐ d. comparison of the American and Russian navies.   _____

Vocabulary in Context

6 Desperate means

☐ a. in great need.

☐ b. reckless.

☐ c. hopeless.

☐ d. skillful.   _____

Add your scores for questions 1-6. Enter the total here and on the graph on page 236.   **Total Score** ☐

30

Let's Shake on It

What could be simpler than shaking fruit from a tree? Well, the job is a lot tougher than you might think. There is definitely a right way and a wrong way to shake a fruit tree. And a person who is a good apple tree shaker may not be a good cherry tree shaker. Different fruits take different shakes.

As a rule, a slow hard shake is best. This makes the fruit fall much faster than a light, quick jiggle. Most fruits have a <u>set</u> number of shakes per minute that will do the best job of getting them out of the tree and onto the ground. To shake down plums, try shaking the tree four hundred times per minute, moving the tree two inches at each shake. Experts say you'll get three times more fruit from the tree than you will if you shake eleven hundred times per minute at one inch per shake. Cherries, because they are smaller, need more jarring. A good rate of shaking seems to be about twelve hundred shakes per minute. Apples, like plums, need four hundred shakes.

Of course, some folks may choose to ignore all these expert directions for jiggling fruit. Keeping track of all the numbers can be enough to drive some people up a tree.

		Answer	Score
Main Idea	1		
	Mark the *main idea* ⟶	M	15
	Mark the statement that is *too broad* ⟶	B	5
	Mark the statement that is *too narrow* ⟶	N	5

a. Some tasks are more complicated than they look. ☐ _____

b. Shaking fruit trees can be a real art. ☐ _____

c. Different fruits require different amounts of shaking. ☐ _____

Score 15 points for each correct answer.   **Score**

Subject Matter

2 This passage is concerned with

☐ a. eating plums.

☐ b. how to shake fruit from a tree.

☐ c. the value of fruits and vegetables.

☐ d. ways in which people shake.

_____

Supporting Details

3 A smaller fruit normally requires

☐ a. a ladder.

☐ b. less shaking.

☐ c. two people per tree.

☐ d. more shaking.

_____

Conclusion

4 From this passage we can conclude that

☐ a. good fruit pickers know how fast or slow to shake a tree.

☐ b. most of the fruits are badly bruised when they hit the ground.

☐ c. it really makes no difference how you shake a fruit tree.

☐ d. too much shaking can damage the branches.

_____

Clarifying Devices

5 The writer ends this story with

☐ a. a serious thought.

☐ b. a suggestion for other ways to get fruit from trees.

☐ c. a joke.

☐ d. a warning.

_____

Vocabulary in Context

6 The word <u>set</u> means

☐ a. tiresome.

☐ b. great.

☐ c. fixed.

☐ d. collected.

_____

Add your scores for questions 1-6. Enter the total here and on the graph on page 236.

Total Score ☐

31

No Laughing Matter

Never laugh at a snow covered mountain! Laughter and yelling, during the avalanche season, can trigger a deadly pile of snow. Huge snow slides are most common in mountains where there are steep slopes that are well buried in snow and ice. The snow builds up slowly and lands very softly. This can create a very touchy, <u>unstable</u> situation. Tons of snow may be held up by only the friction between snowflakes. The deep snow is like a house of cards. The slightest movement can cause it to tumble. As soon as something slips, this great mass of snow will come crashing down the mountainside.

Slides may be started by sound vibrations. They may also be started by the weight of wet, melting snow. Once an avalanche has been triggered, the cause no longer matters. Moving down a steep slope, it picks up great speed and added snow. Some avalanches travel as fast as two hundred miles per hour. The force of an avalanche will mow down anything in its path. Whole houses have been swallowed up by these fast-paced piles of snow.

The wind that is caused by an avalanche is almost as destructive as the snow itself. Winds from an avalanche have been known to travel as fast as those of a tornado. So, when approaching a thickly snow covered mountain, speak softly!

Main Idea   1

	Answer	Score
Mark the *main idea* ⟶	**M**	15
Mark the statement that is *too broad* ⟶	**B**	5
Mark the statement that is *too narrow* ⟶	**N**	5

a. Mountain areas can be very dangerous. ☐ ____

b. Sound vibrations can trigger an avalanche. ☐ ____

c. Avalanches, which are huge piles of tumbling snow, are very dangerous. ☐ ____

Subject Matter

2 This passage is concerned with
- ☐ a. avalanches.
- ☐ b. bad snowstorms.
- ☐ c. mountains.
- ☐ d. laughter.   _____

Supporting Details

3 Avalanches can be started by
- ☐ a. falling snow.
- ☐ b. the wind.
- ☐ c. loud sounds.
- ☐ d. friction between snowflakes.   _____

Conclusion

4 We can conclude from this passage that avalanches
- ☐ a. are common everywhere.
- ☐ b. are not very common.
- ☐ c. have killed people.
- ☐ d. are a thing of the past.   _____

Clarifying Devices

5 The writer compares an avalanche to
- ☐ a. a tornado.
- ☐ b. a falling house of cards.
- ☐ c. a snowstorm.
- ☐ d. a speeding train.   _____

Vocabulary in Context

6 In this passage <u>unstable</u> means
- ☐ a. frightening.
- ☐ b. fast.
- ☐ c. shaky.
- ☐ d. undesirable.   _____

Add your scores for questions 1-6. Enter the total here and on the graph on page 236.   **Total Score** ☐

32

The Geoduck

There's one sure way to work up an appetite for seafood: go digging for the elusive geoduck. Although it sounds as though it should have feathers and webbed feet, a geoduck is a type of clam found on the Pacific Coast. The geoduck is no normal clam. It may grow to be eight inches long. Some have been known to tip the <u>scales</u> at as much as sixteen pounds. But geoducks aren't dredged from the sea's floor, like scallops. They can't even be dug up with a clam rake. If you want to find a geoduck you have to dig and dig and dig.

Like the much smaller soft-shelled clams, the geoduck digs down into soft sand or mud. But instead of hiding a few inches below the surface, the geoduck tunnels much deeper. In fact, it may tunnel as much as three feet down. It sticks its long neck up the trench to the surface to breathe and eat. When disturbed, it can snap its neck back into the shell faster than you can dig. This disappearing act has led some people to conclude that you can't catch a clam that "digs that fast." These people don't realize that the geoduck just pulls its neck down a burrow that already exists. When it comes to digging a new burrow, a geoduck really isn't very fast.

Main Idea	1		Answer	Score
	Mark the *main idea*	→	M	15
	Mark the statement that is *too broad*	→	B	5
	Mark the statement that is *too narrow*	→	N	5

a. Clams like to dig. ☐ ____

b. Geoducks are large clams. ☐ ____

c. Geoducks are big clams that dig very deep burrows. ☐ ____

Score 15 points for each correct answer.

Subject Matter   **2**   This passage is about

☐ a. sandy beaches.

☐ b. a kind of clam.

☐ c. creatures that dig.

☐ d. the tides.

_____

Supporting Details   **3**   Geoducks normally dig

☐ a. in the middle of the night.

☐ b. in soft sand or mud.

☐ c. with a clam rake.

☐ d. shallow holes.

_____

Conclusion   **4**   We can conclude from this passage that the geoduck

☐ a. is a good swimmer.

☐ b. is nearly extinct.

☐ c. is related to geese and ducks.

☐ d. takes practice to catch.

_____

Clarifying Devices   **5**   To explain how geoducks are different from ordinary soft-shelled clams, the writer

☐ a. gives a detailed description of the characteristics of a geoduck.

☐ b. tells a story about a geoduck and a soft-shelled clam.

☐ c. compares and contrasts the two kinds of clams.

☐ d. ignores their similarities.

_____

Vocabulary in Context   **6**   <u>Scales,</u> in this passage, means

☐ a. climbs.

☐ b. the skin covering of fish.

☐ c. a device for weighing.

☐ d. a succession of notes in music.

_____

Add your scores for questions 1–6. Enter the total here and on the graph on page 236.

Total Score ☐

33

People from Outer Space

What do aliens from outer space look like?

They have light grey skin and long oval heads. Their eyes are almond-shaped and their mouths are lipless slits. They have only three fingers on their hands. This is how Betty Hill, under hypnosis, described the creatures who, she says, took her and her husband into their spaceship late one night in 1961.

The Hills were returning home from a visit to Canada. They were driving on a lonely back road when they noticed an eerie light moving over the treetops. It came down in the road ahead of them. Barney Hill hopped out of the car with his binoculars. He could hardly believe what he saw through them. It was a bright pancake-shaped object with a row of windows around the edge. He could see thin figures moving about inside. The next thing he and his wife remember is racing back home in their car.

For over a year after that night, both of the Hills felt nervous and uneasy at odd times. Betty Hill had nightmares about meeting people from outer space. Finally, the couple decided to talk to a UFO (unidentified flying object) investigator. Betty Hill agreed to let a doctor hypnotize her. She then described how the aliens had put her and her husband in a trance and taken them aboard their ship. Once inside, she said, the spacemen examined the Hills with strange instruments. Then they somehow made the couple forget everything. Only under hypnosis could the Hills remember their <u>encounter</u> with the visitors from outer space.

Main Idea	1		Answer	Score
		Mark the *main idea* ⟶	**M**	15
		Mark the statement that is *too broad* ⟶	**B**	5
		Mark the statement that is *too narrow* ⟶	**N**	5
		a. Aliens put the Hills in a trance.	☐	_____
		b. The Hills claim they met aliens from outer space.	☐	_____
		c. Aliens came to study people on earth.	☐	_____

Score 15 points for each correct answer.   **Score**

Subject Matter

2 This passage is mainly about
- ☐ a. hypnosis and memory.
- ☐ b. UFO investigators.
- ☐ c. a visit to Canada.
- ☐ d. visitors from space.

_____

Supporting Details

3 The aliens' spaceship looked like
- ☐ a. an almond.
- ☐ b. a cigar.
- ☐ c. a pancake.
- ☐ d. a saucer.

_____

Conclusion

4 The Hills probably would not have remembered their meeting with the aliens if
- ☐ a. they hadn't been hypnotized.
- ☐ b. they hadn't returned home.
- ☐ c. someone hadn't reminded them.
- ☐ d. the aliens weren't so strange looking.

_____

Clarifying Devices

5 The writer presents the story as though it were
- ☐ a. an argument for the existence of aliens.
- ☐ b. an actual happening.
- ☐ c. an obvious lie.
- ☐ d. a humorous tale.

_____

Vocabulary in Context

6 In this passage, encounter means
- ☐ a. battle.
- ☐ b. kidnapping.
- ☐ c. collision.
- ☐ d. meeting.

_____

Add your scores for questions 1-6. Enter the total here and on the graph on page 236.

Total Score ☐

34

No Chance To Dream

The thought of not sleeping for twenty-four hours or more is not a pleasant one for most people. The amount of sleep that each person needs varies. In general, each of us needs about eight hours of sleep each day to keep our bodies healthy and happy. Some people, however, can get by with just a few hours of sleep at night.

It doesn't matter when or how much a person sleeps. But, everyone needs some rest to stay alive. Few doctors would have thought that there might be an exception to this. Sleep is, after all, a very basic need. But a man named Al Herpin turned out to be a real exception, for supposedly, he never slept!

Al Herpin was 90 years old when doctors came to his home in New Jersey. They hoped to <u>negate</u> the claims that he never slept. But they were surprised. Though they watched him every hour of the day, they never saw Herpin sleeping. He did not even own a bed. He never needed one.

The closest that Herpin came to resting was to sit in a rocking chair and read a half dozen newspapers. His doctors were baffled by this strange case of permanent insomnia. Herpin offered the only clue to his condition. He remembered some talk about his mother having been injured several days before he had been born. Herpin died at the age of 94, never having slept a wink.

Main Idea	1		Answer	Score
	Mark the *main idea* ⟶	M		15
	Mark the statement that is *too broad* ⟶	B		5
	Mark the statement that is *too narrow* ⟶	N		5

a. Some people don't need to sleep. ☐ _____

b. Al Herpin managed to stay alive without ever sleeping. ☐ _____

c. Everyone needs some rest to stay alive. ☐ _____

Subject Matter **2** This passage centers on

☐ a. dream interpretation.
☐ b. patterns of sleep.
☐ c. Al Herpin's sleepless life.
☐ d. sleep and dreams.

_____

Supporting Details **3** The most likely reason for Herpin's insomnia was

☐ a. his mother's injury before he was born.
☐ b. that he never got tired.
☐ c. his magnificent physical condition.
☐ d. that he got enough rest by rocking.

_____

Conclusion **4** Al Herpin's condition could be regarded as

☐ a. normal.
☐ b. curable.
☐ c. healthful.
☐ d. rare.

_____

Clarifying Devices **5** The expression "get by," in the last sentence of the first paragraph is

☐ a. a confusing expression.
☐ b. a vulgar expression.
☐ c. an everyday expression.
☐ d. an improper expression.

_____

Vocabulary in Context **6** Negate is a synonym for

☐ a. support.
☐ b. disprove.
☐ c. hide.
☐ d. verify.

_____

Add your scores for questions 1-6. Enter the total here and on the graph on page 236.

Total Score ☐

35

Can You Answer This Riddle?

The people of old Greece and Egypt believed in <u>mythology</u>. These stories were mostly about strange creatures. Often, the creatures were part human and part animal. One such creature, the Sphinx, had the head of a woman and the body of a lion. The Sphinx lived high on a mountain peak over which a road passed.

People who traveled that way were never heard from again. Whenever travelers reached the peak of the mountain, the Sphinx would block the road and speak this riddle: "What goes on four feet in the morning, on two feet at noon, and on three feet in the evening?" No traveler in a thousand years had guessed the answer. The Sphinx had eaten them all.

But, one day, a Greek traveler named Oedipus traveled that way. When he came to the pass on the mountain the Sphinx leaped out. With a catlike grin, it asked its terrible riddle. Oedipus, wise with age, knew the answer immediately, but he teased the Sphinx by frowning and shaking his head. These strange actions made the Sphinx tense and upset. Then suddenly Oedipus shot forth the answer. The Sphinx was so upset that it jumped off the mountain to its death.

The answer Oedipus gave was one word: man. Can you guess why this was right? In man's morning, or childhood, he crawls on all fours. At noon, as an adult, he walks on two legs. In the evening, old age, he uses a third foot—a cane.

Main Idea	1		Answer	Score
	Mark the *main idea* ⟶	M		15
	Mark the statement that is *too broad* ⟶	B		5
	Mark the statement that is *too narrow* ⟶	N		5

a. The Sphinx asked a riddle that only Oedipus could answer. ☐ _____

b. Greek and Egyptian myths contain stories of many strange creatures. ☐ _____

c. The Sphinx asked a difficult riddle of all travelers who passed by. ☐ _____

Score 15 points for each correct answer.   **Score**

Subject Matter

2 Another good title for this passage would be
- ☐ a. The History of Greece.
- ☐ b. The Sphinx and Its Riddle.
- ☐ c. Mythical Beasts of Greece and Egypt.
- ☐ d. Oedipus and His Riddle.   _____

Supporting Details

3 The Sphinx was
- ☐ a. half man and half woman.
- ☐ b. half woman and half camel.
- ☐ c. half woman and half lion.
- ☐ d. half lion and half horse.   _____

Conclusion

4 The writer suggests that Oedipus was the first to
- ☐ a. see the Sphinx.
- ☐ b. answer the riddle correctly.
- ☐ c. defeat the mighty Sphinx in battle.
- ☐ d. try to answer the riddle.   _____

Clarifying Devices

5 In the Sphinx's riddle, morning, noon, and evening
- ☐ a. are used as symbols.
- ☐ b. have no meaning.
- ☐ c. are used to mean different times of day.
- ☐ d. are the answers to the riddle.   _____

Vocabulary in Context

6 Mythology deals with stories that are
- ☐ a. true.
- ☐ b. historical.
- ☐ c. legendary.
- ☐ d. for children.   _____

Add your scores for questions 1-6. Enter the total here and on the graph on page 236.   **Total Score** ☐

36

The Collapsing Road

Luckily, the back tires of their car stayed on the road. Otherwise, the young couple would have driven right into a pit twenty feet wide and thirty feet deep!

The man and woman were coming home from a party. They were enjoying the landscape around Swansea, Wales. Suddenly, they found the front of their car leaning into a huge hole. The car barely hung on-to the edge of the pit. It swayed back and forth like the arm of a balance.

In their <u>precarious</u> position, the couple knew that each movement they made could be a matter of life and death. Slowly, slowly, they edged toward the backseat. Then each opened a back door. And on the count of three, they jumped out together. The accident was so scary that they ran a long way before they calmed down. But later they returned to see what had happened. They found that a big chunk of the road had sunk into the ground! And at the bottom of the pit lay their car—roof down and wheels up.

Was this mystery of the sunken road ever solved? It turned out that an abandoned mine shaft lay under the road. It had collapsed and taken the pavement with it. Layers of tunnels intersect beneath the city of Swansea. The tunnels were built so many years ago that no one knows where they end or begin. The tunnels are shaky, like those that ants build in the sand. No one knows when the entire city might collapse.

Main Idea 1

	Answer	Score
Mark the *main idea* →	M	15
Mark the statement that is *too broad* →	B	5
Mark the statement that is *too narrow* →	N	5

a. Swansea is built upon a maze of shaky abandoned mine tunnels. ☐ _____

b. Swansea is a very dangerous city to drive in. ☐ _____

c. An abandoned mine tunnel runs directly under one road in Swansea. ☐ _____

Score 15 points for each correct answer. Score

Subject Matter

2 This passage is primarily about
- ☐ a. driving carefully.
- ☐ b. the city of Swansea, Wales.
- ☐ c. a road that caved in.
- ☐ d. tunnels that ants build. _____

Supporting Details

3 According to this selection, the pit was
- ☐ a. a mile wide.
- ☐ b. bottomless.
- ☐ c. part of a volcano.
- ☐ d. thirty feet deep. _____

Conclusion

4 It is probably true that
- ☐ a. the other roads in Swansea are pretty safe.
- ☐ b. other sections of Swansea will cave in sometime.
- ☐ c. everyone should move out of Swansea.
- ☐ d. Swansea is a very interesting city. _____

Clarifying Devices

5 The writer creates interest in the first sentence by using
- ☐ a. a funny story.
- ☐ b. romantic imagery.
- ☐ c. a vivid description.
- ☐ d. a precise argument. _____

Vocabulary in Context

6 The word <u>precarious</u> means
- ☐ a. unexpected.
- ☐ b. dangerous.
- ☐ c. unusual.
- ☐ d. ridiculous. _____

Add your scores for questions 1–6. Enter the total here and on the graph on page 236. Total Score ☐

37

A Whale of a Story

There has been, in history, a man who was swallowed by a whale and lived to tell the tale. The man's name is James Bartley. The records to prove his unusual experience are in the British Admiralty.

Bartley was making his first trip on the whaling ship *Star of the East*. Suddenly the lookout sighted a huge sperm whale. The whalers knew it was a huge whale by the size of the spray it blew into the air. They lowered their small boats. James Bartley was in the first longboat. The men rowed until they were close to the whale. A harpoon was thrown and it found its mark. It sank into the whale's flesh. The maddened beast crashed into the boat, snapping its tail at the men and the wreckage of their boats. When the survivors were picked up, James Bartley was missing.

Shortly before sunset, the whale was finally captured. The sailors tied the whale's <u>carcass</u> to the side of the ship. Because of the hot weather it was important that they cut up the whale right away. Otherwise, the meat would begin to rot and the oil would begin to spoil. When they got to the stomach, they felt something moving about wildly. They thought it would be a big fish still alive inside. But when they opened the stomach they found James Bartley. After this trip, Bartley settled in Gloucester, England, and never returned to sea.

Main Idea	1		Answer	Score
		Mark the *main idea* ⟶	M	15
		Mark the statement that is *too broad* ⟶	B	5
		Mark the statement that is *too narrow* ⟶	N	5
		a. Whaling was a dangerous business.	☐	___
		b. A whale smashed a small boat from the whaling ship.	☐	___
		c. James Bartley was swallowed by a whale and lived.	☐	___

Score

Subject Matter

2 This passage is mainly about

☐ a. how to hunt whales for their oil and meat.

☐ b. the hard and dangerous lives that whalers had to live.

☐ c. the duties of each man on a whaling ship.

☐ d. a man who was swallowed by a whale and lived.

_____

Supporting Details

3 The sailors knew that something was in the whale's stomach because

☐ a. they could feel it moving about wildly.

☐ b. the whale seemed very heavy.

☐ c. the whale was bulging out at one spot.

☐ d. the captain heard Bartley yelling for help.

_____

Conclusion

4 James Bartley probably never went to sea again because

☐ a. he wanted different kinds of adventures.

☐ b. of fright and shock.

☐ c. he was crippled by the whale.

☐ d. he often got seasick.

_____

Clarifying Devices

5 The author, in telling James Bartley's story, informs us by

☐ a. narrating the plain facts.

☐ b. referring to whaling in general.

☐ c. comparing whaling to other fishing.

☐ d. dramatically telling what happened.

_____

Vocabulary in Context

6 The word carcass refers to the

☐ a. whale's tail.

☐ b. whale's blubber.

☐ c. dead body of the whale.

☐ d. whale's side.

_____

Add your scores for questions 1-6. Enter the total here and on the graph on page 236.

Total Score ☐

38

The World's Oldest Sport

Most of us have heard of thoroughbred horses. But what does "thoroughbred" mean? It means a horse of a pure breed. This is a type of horse that has not been mixed with any other type of horse through breeding. Thoroughbred horses are the world's fastest racers. Long ago, three Arabian stallions were brought to Britain by King Charles II. They were the ancestors of all thoroughbreds known today. They could run like lightning. They also had very unusual names. They were called Byerley Turk, Godolphin Barb and Darley Arabian.

Horse racing is one of the oldest sports in the world. Rulers of all times have enjoyed breeding their own horses. In the Middle Ages, kings liked to watch their knights on horseback compete in tournaments. Because of this, horse racing is often called "the sport of kings."

There are many different kinds of horse races. Flat races are races that take place on grass or dirt tracks. They are called "flat" because the horse is not made to jump over any obstacles.

In another kind of race, called the steeplechase, a horse must jump at least eighteen fences! Steeplechasing gets its name from races once held in Ireland. In these events, the course was set between the church steeples of one village and the next. The most famous steeplechase in modern times is the Grand National, held in Britain.

	1		Answer	Score
Main Idea				
	Mark the *main idea* ⟶	**M**		15
	Mark the statement that is *too broad* ⟶	**B**		5
	Mark the statement that is *too narrow* ⟶	**N**		5

a. Thoroughbreds are the fastest horses in the world. ☐ _____

b. People have used horses for many purposes. ☐ _____

c. Horse racing is one of the oldest sports in the world. ☐ _____

Score 15 points for each correct answer.   **Score**

Subject Matter

2 This passage is mostly about
- ☐ a. the Middle Ages.
- ☐ b. Arabian stallions.
- ☐ c. horse racing.
- ☐ d. steeplechasing.

_____

Supporting Details

3 Steeplechasing gets its name from
- ☐ a. races once held in Ireland.
- ☐ b. horses that run toward steeples.
- ☐ c. horses that run away from steeples.
- ☐ d. horses that jump over high obstacles.

_____

Conclusion

4 From this passage, we can see that
- ☐ a. horse racing is a sport that only royalty enjoy.
- ☐ b. horses love to race.
- ☐ c. horse racing has been popular for a long time.
- ☐ d. horse racing is only enjoyed in Britain.

_____

Clarifying Devices

5 "They could run like lightning" means the horses were
- ☐ a. unpredictable.
- ☐ b. electrifying.
- ☐ c. dangerous.
- ☐ d. fast.

_____

Vocabulary in Context

6 An <u>ancestor</u> is
- ☐ a. a very close relative.
- ☐ b. a thoroughbred horse.
- ☐ c. a relative who lived long ago.
- ☐ d. a horse that is very fast.

_____

Add your scores for questions 1-6. Enter the total here and on the graph on page 236.

Total Score ☐

39

Perchance to Dream

Need some sleep? Maybe you should try curling up in a cactus. This prickly plant can provide sound slumber. It's worked as a bedroom for the desert centipede for years. The centipede is a long bug with one hundred legs. Although pretty scary to look at itself, the bug is afraid of the tarantula, a large dark spider with eight big hairy legs.

Each night before the centipede goes to sleep, it builds a special burglar alarm made of cactus. It surrounds itself with these sharp plants. The smart bug knows that the tarantula will never crawl over cactus. That would be like hugging a porcupine. So the centipede sleeps safely in its cactus corral. It can be sure that no enemy will get in.

Shut out by this prickly prison, the hungry tarantula lurks outside the centipede's bedroom for hours. First it circles the wall, then it peers over and circles again. Finally it decides that there is nothing it can do. It leaves the centipede to sleep and goes off to look for a creature that won't protect itself as well.

The next day the centipede wakes up from a good night's sleep. The tarantula has surely given up by now. Still, the centipede is <u>cautious</u>. It takes a long and very careful look around. Only when it's sure that the coast is clear does the centipede begin to remove the wall of cactus that protected it in sleep.

Main Idea	1		Answer	Score
		Mark the *main idea* ⟶	**M**	15
		Mark the statement that is *too broad* ⟶	**B**	5
		Mark the statement that is *too narrow* ⟶	**N**	5

a. The tarantula will not climb over cactus. ☐ _____

b. Some creatures have unique methods of protecting themselves. ☐ _____

c. Centipedes protect themselves when they sleep by surrounding themselves with a wall of cactus. ☐ _____

Subject Matter　**2**　This passage is about

☐ a. the danger of tarantulas.

☐ b. creatures of the desert.

☐ c. the centipede's unique form of protection.

☐ d. how to get to sleep.　　　　_____

Supporting Details　**3**　Despite their excellent forts, centipedes are still very

☐ a. small.

☐ b. slow.

☐ c. cautious.

☐ d. reckless.　　　　_____

Conclusion　**4**　We can conclude that tarantulas

☐ a. don't eat centipedes.

☐ b. are related to porcupines.

☐ c. try to attack centipedes every night.

☐ d. are smarter than centipedes.　　　　_____

Clarifying Devices　**5**　The writer compares climbing on cactus to

☐ a. walking over hot coals.

☐ b. going without eating for weeks.

☐ c. hugging a porcupine.

☐ d. sleeping on a pin cushion.　　　　_____

Vocabulary in Context　**6**　A centipede that is <u>cautious</u> is

☐ a. careful.

☐ b. afraid.

☐ c. fearsome.

☐ d. poisonous.　　　　_____

Add your scores for questions 1-6. Enter the total here and on the graph on page 236.　　**Total Score** ☐

40

Abe's Favorite Story

If he hadn't turned to politics, Abe Lincoln might have done well as a comic. It has been said that he was always ready to join in a laugh at his own expense. There is one particular story that he always told with great glee.

In his early days as a lawyer, Lincoln was on the "circuit." This meant going from town to town to hear and judge legal cases. During one of these many trips, he was sitting in a train when a strange man came up to him. The stranger looked at the tall gawky lawyer quite sternly and explained that he had something he believed belonged to Lincoln. Lincoln was a bit confused. He had never seen the man before. He didn't see how a total stranger could have something of his. Lincoln asked him how this could be. The stranger pulled out a gleaming pen knife and began to explain. Many years before, he had been given the pocket knife. He had been told to keep it until he was able to find a man uglier than himself.

Lincoln's eyes always sparkled when he reached this part of the story. He was never considered a handsome man. The stranger had decided that Lincoln was ugly enough to deserve the knife. The story always brought smiles to the faces of the audience that heard it. The tale itself was funny. But even more delightful was the fact that a man as great as Lincoln could still laugh at himself.

Main Idea   1

	Answer	Score
Mark the *main idea* ⟶	M	15
Mark the statement that is *too broad* ⟶	B	5
Mark the statement that is *too narrow* ⟶	N	5

a. Abe Lincoln used to tell a funny story that showed he could laugh at himself. ☐ _____

b. A good sense of humor can be a rare gift. ☐ _____

c. Lincoln's story makes fun of his ugliness. ☐ _____

**Subject
Matter**

2 This passage is about

☐ a. Abe Lincoln's legal practice.

☐ b. a funny story that Abe Lincoln used to tell.

☐ c. the value of a pen knife.

☐ d. traveling on trains.   _____

**Supporting
Details**

3 As a tribute to his ugliness, Lincoln was given a

☐ a. handshake.

☐ b. good laugh.

☐ c. pen knife.

☐ d. train ticket.   _____

Conclusion

4 We can conclude that Lincoln's good sense of humor

☐ a. was frowned upon by most.

☐ b. made him a more popular person.

☐ c. was developed when he was a traveling lawyer.

☐ d. was the reason he was elected president.   _____

**Clarifying
Devices**

5 This passage

☐ a. gives many facts about Lincoln.

☐ b. gives a short history lesson.

☐ c. tells a story.

☐ d. is a fable.   _____

**Vocabulary
in Context**

6 In this passage the word expense means

☐ a. price.

☐ b. amount of money.

☐ c. charge.

☐ d. loss, or sacrifice.   _____

**Add your scores for questions 1-6. Enter the
total here and on the graph on page 236.**   **Total
Score** [ ]

41

Peanuts and Protein

Is that a goober in your goulash? The lowly peanut, called the goober in some places, will soon be used in many new ways as a boost to our diets. Peanut butter, salted peanuts and peanut oil are already used in many candies and snacks. But peanuts are more than just snacks. They are also very good for you. In fact, few foods are richer in protein. Now, new ways of using the peanut's natural proteins are being developed.

Peanut flakes are among the latest ideas. After being boiled, chopped, dried and ground, these flakes no longer taste like peanuts. Instead, they have a <u>bland</u> neutral flavor. This makes them perfect for slipping into other foods as a nutrient. Peanuts are one third protein. What's more, they're relatively cheap. This means they can be used in place of more expensive sources of protein such as meat and fish. Peanut flakes absorb the taste of the foods they are cooked with. Scramble them with eggs, and the flakes double the nutritional value of the eggs. Yet, your eggs will still taste like eggs. Flakes can be mixed in with cereals or pressed into high protein crackers. Peanuts can even be used as a substitute for beef in many recipes.

Main Idea   1

	Answer	Score
Mark the *main idea* ⟶	M	15
Mark the statement that is *too broad* ⟶	B	5
Mark the statement that is *too narrow* ⟶	N	5
a. Peanut flakes are made from peanuts.	☐	___
b. Peanut flakes are a good protein supplement.	☐	___
c. Peanuts are very nutritious.	☐	___

Score 15 points for each correct answer.   Score

Subject Matter

2 This passage focuses on peanut
- ☐ a. butter.
- ☐ b. flakes.
- ☐ c. oil.
- ☐ d. cereal.   _____

Supporting Details

3 Peanut flakes
- ☐ a. are white in color.
- ☐ b. are not found in nature.
- ☐ c. don't even taste like peanuts.
- ☐ d. don't taste good.   _____

Conclusion

4 We can conclude from this passage that
- ☐ a. peanut flakes will soon be used in many foods.
- ☐ b. other nuts are also high in protein.
- ☐ c. peanut butter is not very tasty.
- ☐ d. peanuts are not as good for you as meat and fish.   _____

Clarifying Devices

5 In the second paragraph, the phrase "what's more" is
- ☐ a. used for emphasis.
- ☐ b. another way of saying "not only that."
- ☐ c. a question of size.
- ☐ d. another way of saying "unfortunately."   _____

Vocabulary in Context

6 Bland means
- ☐ a. unpleasant.
- ☐ b. spicy.
- ☐ c. strong.
- ☐ d. mild.   _____

Add your scores for questions 1-6. Enter the total here and on the graph on page 237.

Total Score ☐

42

No Runs, No Hits and Too Many Errors

Some days it just doesn't pay to go to the ball park. One day in 1966, Los Angeles Dodger outfielder Willie Davis was thinking of places that he'd rather have been. At the time, anywhere must have seemed more inviting. The game he would like to have skipped was no ordinary contest. It was the World Series.

1966 had been a good year for the Dodgers. They had clinched the National League Pennant with ease. All that was left was the World Series against the Baltimore Orioles. As far as most fans and sportswriters were concerned, the "Fall Classic" would be no contest. The Dodgers had powerful hitting and a pitcher who threw the ball so fast that some people insisted it could cause a sonic boom. But something unexpected happened. The Orioles' pitching sparkled. Their hitters were slugging the ball over the outfield fences. All the Dodger fans could talk about was the "cold Dodger bats," that is when they weren't talking about Willie Davis and "that inning." In this particular game Davis set a major league record, one that no ball player would be proud of. In one short inning he made three errors. He let an easy hit skid by him. Several pitches later, he lost a fly in the glare of the sun. And if that wasn't bad enough, he picked up the ball he had missed and threw it over the infielder's head. Davis felt bad, but he wasn't alone. The Dodgers lost the best-out-of-seven series without winning a single game.

Main Idea 1

	Answer	Score
Mark the *main idea*	M	15
Mark the statement that is *too broad*	B	5
Mark the statement that is *too narrow*	N	5

a. Willie Davis had a bad day.

b. Davis set a record by making three errors in one World Series inning.

c. Willie Davis played for the Los Angeles Dodgers in the World Series.

Score 15 points for each correct answer. Score

Subject Matter

2 This passage deals with
- ☐ a. baseball fielding lessons.
- ☐ b. a bad dream.
- ☐ c. an unfortunate major league record.
- ☐ d. the city of Los Angeles. _____

Supporting Details

3 Davis couldn't catch one of the fly balls because of
- ☐ a. a back problem.
- ☐ b. the glare of the sun.
- ☐ c. a hole in his mitt.
- ☐ d. another fielder who got in the way. _____

Conclusion

4 From reading this passage, we can conclude that, because of his mistakes that day, Willie Davis was
- ☐ a. thrown off the team.
- ☐ b. arrested.
- ☐ c. embarrassed.
- ☐ d. ignored by his teammates. _____

Clarifying Devices

5 The term "cold Dodger bats" refers to
- ☐ a. poor hitting.
- ☐ b. winter weather that canceled a game.
- ☐ c. a new technique of cooling the baseball bats.
- ☐ d. flying creatures which plague Dodger Stadium. _____

Vocabulary in Context

6 In this passage, record means
- ☐ a. to put on tape.
- ☐ b. a disc with music on it.
- ☐ c. a performance surpassing all others.
- ☐ d. a written document. _____

Add your scores for questions 1-6. Enter the total here and on the graph on page 237.

Total Score ☐

107

43

Are You Superstitious?

Many superstitious people are afraid of black cats. They believe that black cats have a strange power. If a black cat crosses their path, they think they will have bad luck.

Black cats haven't always had such a bad reputation. Long ago, the Egyptians thought that black cats were holy animals. They even worshipped them. Pasht was an Egyptian goddess who had a woman's body and a cat's head. Because the Egyptians had so much respect for black cats, they often buried the <u>sacred</u> creatures with great ceremony. Mummies of cats have often been found in ancient cemetery ruins. To keep the cats company after they died, mice were sometimes buried beside them.

Feelings about black cats have always been strong. People have thought they were either very good or very bad. The people of Europe, in the Middle Ages, believed black cats were the evil friends of witches and the Devil. Witches were said to have the power to change themselves into black cats. People believed that you could not tell whether a black cat was just a cat, or whether it was a witch disguising herself as she plotted some evil scheme. The brain of a black cat was thought to be a main ingredient in witch's brew.

Unlike their ancestors of the Middle Ages, Englishmen today consider black cats to be good luck charms. Fishermen's wives often keep a black cat around so that their husbands will be protected when they are out at sea.

Main Idea	1		Answer	Score
	Mark the *main idea*	→	M	15
	Mark the statement that is *too broad*	→	B	5
	Mark the statement that is *too narrow*	→	N	5

a. People think that cats are special animals. ☐ _____

b. Black cats have always been thought to have special powers. ☐ _____

c. Superstitious people believe that black cats bring bad luck. ☐ _____

Score 15 points for each correct answer. Score

Subject Matter

2 The subject of this passage is
- ☐ a. witches.
- ☐ b. superstition.
- ☐ c. black cats.
- ☐ d. ancient beliefs. _____

Supporting Details

3 The Egyptian goddess Pasht had a
- ☐ a. woman's head and a cat's body.
- ☐ b. woman's head and a lion's body.
- ☐ c. cat's head and a man's body.
- ☐ d. woman's body and a cat's head. _____

Conclusion

4 Judging from this passage, people of the Middle Ages probably
- ☐ a. treated black cats with respect.
- ☐ b. treated black cats badly.
- ☐ c. were witches if they had black cats.
- ☐ d. thought black cats were beautiful. _____

Clarifying Devices

5 People of ancient Egypt and Europeans of the Middle Ages
- ☐ a. both worshipped black cats.
- ☐ b. both feared black cats.
- ☐ c. thought black cats could bring good luck.
- ☐ d. felt very differently about black cats. _____

Vocabulary in Context

6 Sacred means
- ☐ a. dead.
- ☐ b. holy.
- ☐ c. black.
- ☐ d. fearful. _____

Add your scores for questions 1-6. Enter the total here and on the graph on page 237. Total Score ☐

44

Scallops and Clams

Scallops and clams are both mollusks—shelled sea creatures with soft bodies. Yet, they have more differences than similarities. Scallops and clams both feed by pulling water through their shells and straining out tiny plants and animals as their food. Both shellfish are popular prey for many other sea creatures. But when it comes to searching for safety, they have very different ways.

The scallop lies on the floor of the ocean in shallow to fairly deep water. Its curved shell raises it just above the sand or gravel on the bottom. It looks almost helpless lying there. But don't let it fool you. There is a ring of tiny eyes peering out from the scallop's shell. At the first sign of a predator, the scallop takes off, swimming by <u>jetting</u> spurts of water out behind it. It's a very fast swimmer.

Any clam that dared to lie in full view on the ocean floor would quickly be eaten. Clams make a tasty meal for starfish, crabs or carnivorous snails. They move very slowly and cannot swim at all. They find safety by burrowing deep into the mud or sand. Their long necks stretch like periscopes, up to the top of the sand. Just the tip of the neck pokes out to get food for the clam. If anything comes near, the neck can quickly be pulled back within the shell. The clam stays safe below the surface, two or three feet down.

Main Idea	1		Answer	Score
		Mark the *main idea* ⟶	**M**	15
		Mark the statement that is *too broad* ⟶	**B**	5
		Mark the statement that is *too narrow* ⟶	**N**	5

a. Scallops and clams live on the ocean floor. ☐ _____

b. Scallops and clams use different methods to defend themselves. ☐ _____

c. Scallops and clams are good prey for many other ocean creatures. ☐ _____

Score 15 points for each correct answer.   Score

Subject Matter

2 This passage focuses on
- ☐ a. predators of clams and scallops.
- ☐ b. how scallops and clams protect themselves.
- ☐ c. the similarities between scallops and clams.
- ☐ d. how scallops and clams feed.   _____

Supporting Details

3 Clams and scallops eat
- ☐ a. fish.
- ☐ b. crabs.
- ☐ c. tiny plants and animals.
- ☐ d. water.   _____

Conclusion

4 Based on this passage, which statement is most likely to be true?
- ☐ a. Scallops are smarter than clams.
- ☐ b. A clam has no need for eyes.
- ☐ c. Scallops have longer necks than clams.
- ☐ d. Clams are more cowardly than scallops.   _____

Clarifying Devices

5 The writer compares a clam's neck to
- ☐ a. a giraffe's neck.
- ☐ b. a skyscraper.
- ☐ c. a snorkel.
- ☐ d. a periscope.   _____

Vocabulary in Context

6 Jetting means
- ☐ a. squirting.
- ☐ b. exploding.
- ☐ c. flying.
- ☐ d. leaving.   _____

Add your scores for questions 1-6. Enter the total here and on the graph on page 237.

Total
Score [____]

45

Into Thin Air

"They always get their man." The Royal Canadian Mounted Police are the leaders of Canadian law enforcement. They have always been proud of the fact that they usually find who they are looking for. There was one bizarre case though, where they lost an entire village. A whole community of Eskimo men, women and children vanished without a trace. They were never to be found. The village, Lake Angikuni, was a winter campsite for a tribe of Eskimos. It was close to the hunting grounds but far enough away from civilization that the people could live in peace. A French Canadian named Joe LaBelle often visited the tribe. He shared news, ate caribou, smoked pipes of tobacco and swapped furs with the people.

One day in November of 1930, Joe got to the village and noticed something strange. Normally, Lake Angikuni was alive with the sounds of adults working and children playing. Now it was silent. He looked in the tents and found they were all empty. It appeared as though everyone in the village had left abruptly. A mother had left a bone needle sticking in a piece of cloth as though she had stopped suddenly in the middle of sewing. More shocking to Joe was the fact that the prized rifles had been left behind. He knew the guns were the most valued possessions of the Eskimos. Joe informed the Mounties, but to this day they have been unable to find even one person from the village.

			Answer	Score
Main Idea	1			
		Mark the *main idea* ⟶	M	15
		Mark the statement that is *too broad* ⟶	B	5
		Mark the statement that is *too narrow* ⟶	N	5

a. Eskimo villagers left their homes mysteriously and have never been found. ☐ _____

b. The Eskimo village of Angikuni was a winter campsite. ☐ _____

c. An unusual event took place in a remote Eskimo village. ☐ _____

Score 15 points for each correct answer.   Score

Subject Matter

2 Another good title for this passage would be
- ☐ a. The Village That Disappeared.
- ☐ b. The Royal Canadian Mounted Police.
- ☐ c. The Life of a Trapper.
- ☐ d. The Eskimo Way of Life.   _____

Supporting Details

3 The Eskimos' most favored belongings were their
- ☐ a. sleds.
- ☐ b. pipes.
- ☐ c. furs.
- ☐ d. rifles.   _____

Conclusion

4 We can assume that the Mounties
- ☐ a. gave up looking for the villagers after a few days.
- ☐ b. looked long and hard for the villagers who disappeared.
- ☐ c. were surprised that the villagers didn't take their sewing.
- ☐ d. were afraid after this strange occurrence.   _____

Clarifying Devices

5 The writer begins the first paragraph with
- ☐ a. a joke.
- ☐ b. a story.
- ☐ c. a slogan.
- ☐ d. a riddle.   _____

Vocabulary in Context

6 Abruptly means
- ☐ a. sadly.
- ☐ b. slowly.
- ☐ c. suddenly.
- ☐ d. in anger.   _____

Add your scores for questions 1-6. Enter the total here and on the graph on page 237.   Total Score ☐

46

Monkey Do

Would you send a monkey to do your shopping for you? Sounds pretty strange, doesn't it? But monkeys can be trained to do some amazing things. Most people are aware that monkeys are one of nature's brainier beasts. Scientists have been studying the link between monkeys and people for a long time. They have designed experiments that test the monkey's ability to perform simple human tasks.

In one test, a Southern psychologist put two monkeys in cages beside each other. Each cage contained a vending machine. One cage had a machine which gave out water. The other had one which gave out food. Instead of real coins, each monkey was given a bag of black and white tokens. The black tokens worked only in the food machine. The white tokens worked in the machine with the water. In time, both animals were able to figure out which coin worked in which machine.

Then the test was made harder. The coins were taken away. The monkey with the water machine was not allowed to have any water for twenty-four hours. The food monkey was deprived of food. The next day, the coins were returned to the monkeys. This time, though, the monkey with the food machine was given water machine tokens, and the monkey with the water machine was given the tokens that worked the food machine. What did the two hungry monkeys do? These smart creatures simply reached through the bars of their cages and traded tokens.

Main Idea	1		Answer	Score
		Mark the *main idea* ⟶	**M**	15
		Mark the statement that is *too broad* ⟶	**B**	5
		Mark the statement that is *too narrow* ⟶	**N**	5

a. An experiment showed that monkeys are capable of reasoning intelligently. ☐ _____

b. Some animals are very smart. ☐ _____

c. Scientists have experimented with monkeys for a long time. ☐ _____

Score 15 points for each correct answer.

Score

Subject Matter

2 This passage deals with

☐ a. vending machines.

☐ b. an experiment with monkeys.

☐ c. monkeys that go shopping.

☐ d. why animals are kept in cages.

_____

Supporting Details

3 The black tokens worked for

☐ a. both machines.

☐ b. the food machine one day and the water machine the next.

☐ c. only the food machine.

☐ d. only the water machine.

_____

Conclusion

4 This experiment showed that monkeys can

☐ a. trick the scientists.

☐ b. survive without food and water for a day.

☐ c. solve problems.

☐ d. share with each other.

_____

Clarifying Devices

5 Most of the passage is devoted to

☐ a. an experiment.

☐ b. a strange story.

☐ c. a joke.

☐ d. advice.

_____

Vocabulary in Context

6 In this passage, <u>link</u> means

☐ a. ring of a chain.

☐ b. problem.

☐ c. connection.

☐ d. differences.

_____

Add your scores for questions 1-6. Enter the total here and on the graph on page 237.

Total Score ☐

47

The Octopus Plant

Unless you have visited the southern United States, you probably have never heard of kudzu. Kudzu, as any southern farmer will sadly tell you, is a super-powered weed. It is a strong climbing vine. Once it gets started, kudzu is almost impossible to stop. It climbs to the tops of the tallest trees. It can cover large buildings. Whole barns and farm houses have been known to disappear from view. It has even been said to engulf small, slow-moving children, but that is probably an exaggeration. Still, wherever it grows, its thick, twisting vines are hard to remove.

Kudzu was once thought to be a helpful plant. Originally found in Asia, it was brought to America to help fight erosion. It was planted where its tough roots, which grow up to five feet long, could help hold back the soil. But the plant soon spread to places where it wasn't wanted. Farmers now have to fight to keep it from eating up all the nutrients in the soil and killing other plants. It has become a sign of unemployment in the South; where there is no one to work the fields, kudzu soon takes over.

The northern United States faces no threat from kudzu. Harsh winters kill off its vines. It loves the warmth of the South. But the South surely doesn't love it. If someone could invent some use for kudzu, and take it off southern farmers' lands, their fortune would be assured.

Main Idea	1		Answer	Score
	Mark the *main idea* ⟶	M		15
	Mark the statement that is *too broad* ⟶	B		5
	Mark the statement that is *too narrow* ⟶	N		5

a. Kudzu is a plant that was used to help fight soil erosion. ☐ _____

b. Kudzu is a fast-growing vine that has become a pest in the southern U.S. ☐ _____

c. Southern farmers face many difficulties in raising crops. ☐ _____

Score 15 points for each correct answer.

Subject   **2** This passage is mostly concerned with
Matter
    ☐ a. kudzu.
    ☐ b. farming.
    ☐ c. the South.
    ☐ d. soil erosion.   _____

Supporting **3** When fields are neglected in the South,
Details
    ☐ a. erosion becomes a problem.
    ☐ b. farmers attack the kudzu.
    ☐ c. employment is bound to improve.
    ☐ d. kudzu soon grows over them.   _____

Conclusion **4** We can conclude from the passage that kudzu
    ☐ a. is more helpful than harmful.
    ☐ b. is more harmful than helpful.
    ☐ c. is spreading to the North.
    ☐ d. holds promise as a seasonal food.   _____

Clarifying **5** The author makes a case against kudzu by
Devices
    ☐ a. citing opinions.
    ☐ b. predicting its future.
    ☐ c. describing its effects.
    ☐ d. criticizing its defenders.   _____

Vocabulary **6** The word <u>engulf</u> means
in Context
    ☐ a. take root.
    ☐ b. confuse.
    ☐ c. completely cover.
    ☐ d. carry off.   _____

Add your scores for questions 1-6. Enter the   **Total**
total here and on the graph on page 237.   **Score** ☐

48

Never Say Die

On October 17, 1829, Sam Patch did what he had said he would do. He perched on a platform built beside Niagara Falls, and jumped into the river a hundred feet below. A big crowd had gathered to watch Sam's well-advertised leap. The spectators held their breath as the daredevil hit the swirling water. At last his head burst out of the foam, thirty feet clear of the falls. The crowd let out a mighty roar. Men waved their hats and yelled out the expression that had become Sam's trademark: "There's no mistake in Sam Patch!"

Sam began his career as a leaper in 1827, when he jumped eighty feet into the Passaic River, from a bridge that was still under construction. He was delighted with the notoriety he received. He traveled from town to town, jumping from masts, cliffs and bridges. Then he made his great conquest of Niagara Falls.

Sam was spurred on by the widespread public excitement over his successful leap from the Falls. He turned to the higher Genesee Falls for his next feat. On November 13, a scaffold was constructed 125 feet above the base of the Falls. A huge crowd gathered on both river banks. At 2:00 P.M., Sam climbed the shaky scaffold, made a brief speech, and jumped. Once again there was hushed silence as his body smacked the water. But this time Sam didn't resurface.

Sam's body was pulled from the mouth of the river the following spring. Even so, for years afterward, a legend persisted that the great Sam Patch was still alive.

Main Idea	1		Answer	Score
	Mark the *main idea* ⟶		M	15
	Mark the statement that is *too broad* ⟶		B	5
	Mark the statement that is *too narrow* ⟶		N	5
	a. Sam Patch died jumping the Genesee Falls.		☐	
	b. Jumping from great heights is dangerous.		☐	
	c. Sam Patch made a career of leaping from great heights.		☐	

Score 15 points for each correct answer.

Subject Matter **2** What is the general idea of the passage?

☐ a. Genesee Falls is a dangerous place.

☐ b. Sam Patch jumped at Niagara Falls.

☐ c. There's no mistake in Sam Patch.

☐ d. Sam Patch was a popular leaper.   _____

Supporting Details **3** Sam jumped into the Passaic River from a

☐ a. cliff.

☐ b. scaffold.

☐ c. bridge.

☐ d. mast.   _____

Conclusion **4** The passage implies that

☐ a. Sam Patch is still alive.

☐ b. Sam Patch was a foolish man.

☐ c. jumping from high bridges was not very dangerous.

☐ d. Sam Patch loved to get a lot of attention.   _____

Clarifying Devices **5** "Swirling" water is

☐ a. very rough.

☐ b. cold.

☐ c. boiling.

☐ d. deep.   _____

Vocabulary in Context **6** The best definition for the word <u>notoriety</u> is

☐ a. congratulations.

☐ b. payment.

☐ c. fame.

☐ d. pleasure.   _____

Add your scores for questions 1–6. Enter the total here and on the graph on page 237.

Total Score ☐

49

This Hare Is No Bunny

There would be no room for the water. That's what the ocean might be like if all the sea hares that are born grew up without a hitch. A refreshing splash in the waves would turn into an uncomfortable wade through a mass of shellfish. The sea hare is one of the oddest animals in the sea. It is a snail. And like most snails, it lives close to the shore. It too has a shell, but the sea hare's shell is paper thin. It covers its entire body. This delicate covering gives the sea hare no protection from its enemies. However, scientists think the hare has another form of defense. If a sea hare is <u>disturbed</u>, it shoots a cloud of purple fluid into the water around it. Scientists think that predators find the fluid unpleasant to taste or smell.

Adult sea hares have very few enemies. But baby sea hares have a great deal of trouble surviving. One mother sea hare that was being observed laid five hundred million eggs in the span of five months. If each mother sea hare produced that many eggs, and they all lived, the ocean would be solidly packed with nothing but sea hares. But they don't all survive. Like the young of many animals that give birth to great numbers of babies, most of the eggs and new baby sea hares are eaten. Other animals in the water devour them in huge quantities. Only a few eggs survive and become adults.

Main Idea	1		Answer	Score
		Mark the *main idea* →	M	15
		Mark the statement that is *too broad* →	B	5
		Mark the statement that is *too narrow* →	N	5

a. Sea hares are snails that live close to the ocean shore. ☐ _____

b. Sea hares, which are odd sea snails, lay a great many eggs, but few baby sea hares survive to adulthood. ☐ _____

c. Sea snails are amazing creatures to observe. ☐ _____

Score 15 points for each correct answer. Score

Subject Matter **2** Another good title for this selection would be

☐ a. Snails at Sea.

☐ b. Predators of Sea Hares.

☐ c. A Hare That Doesn't Run.

☐ d. Wonders Along the Ocean Shore. _____

Supporting Details **3** Sea hares shoot out a purple fluid around themselves to

☐ a. tempt predators.

☐ b. kill predators.

☐ c. attract their young.

☐ d. discourage predators. _____

Conclusion **4** We can infer from the passage that

☐ a. an overabundance of sea hares will never be a problem.

☐ b. sea hares have no form of protection.

☐ c. adult sea hares have no enemies.

☐ d. sea hares will soon crowd the ocean. _____

Clarifying Devices **5** By saying "scientists think," the writer implies that the information that follows

☐ a. has not been proven to be true.

☐ b. is not true.

☐ c. is a wild guess.

☐ d. is a fact. _____

Vocabulary in Context **6** A <u>disturbed</u> sea hare is one that

☐ a. has been eaten by an enemy.

☐ b. has been provoked by a predator.

☐ c. has lost its temper.

☐ d. wants to color up the water. _____

Add your scores for questions 1–6. Enter the total here and on the graph on page 237.

Total Score ☐

50

Glass on the Beach

If you've gone to the same seashore for several years, you may have noticed that the beach gets smaller every year. The wind and the waves carry the beach out to sea, bit by bit. Most shore towns try to fight the beach changes caused by ocean currents and the tides. Some dig sand out of backwater bays and dump it on the beachfront. Others build wooden piers and jetties made to keep currents away from the beach.

A type of artificial sand that has been developed might be able to slow down beach erosion. Strangely, this new kind of sand is made of ground glass! You might think that walking barefoot on ground glass would be painful. But it's not. The reason is very simple. Sand and glass are made of the same kind of material, called silicate. When glass is ground very finely, you get a sandlike substance that is harder than real sand. The size of the pieces can be controlled. Larger pieces won't be as easily affected by the wind and waves. So, a beach covered with artificial sand would last longer than a beach with real sand.

A wonderful thing about artificial sand is that it can be made from waste glass. But making artificial sand costs three times as much as using <u>conventional</u> methods of beach protection. So, it is not likely that sand made of glass will be used in the near future.

Main Idea	1		Answer	Score
		Mark the *main idea* ⟶	M	15
		Mark the statement that is *too broad* ⟶	B	5
		Mark the statement that is *too narrow* ⟶	N	5

a. Artificial sand can slow beach erosion. ☐ _____

b. Beaches are washed away by wind and waves. ☐ _____

c. Many things can be used to stop beaches from shrinking. ☐ _____

Score 15 points for each correct answer. Score

Subject Matter **2** The subject of this passage is

☐ a. summer vacations.

☐ b. the seashore.

☐ c. artificial sand.

☐ d. sand and water.

_____

Supporting Details **3** Ground glass is

☐ a. hard to walk on.

☐ b. similar to sand but harder.

☐ c. difficult to make.

☐ d. found in nature.

_____

Conclusion **4** The passage suggests that artificial sand is

☐ a. not nice looking.

☐ b. the best way to slow down erosion.

☐ c. a foolish idea.

☐ d. too costly to ever be used.

_____

Clarifying Devices **5** In the first sentence, the author gets the reader's attention by

☐ a. referring to something the reader might be familiar with.

☐ b. telling a fact that is very humorous.

☐ c. saying something very surprising.

☐ d. asking a question.

_____

Vocabulary in Context **6** <u>Conventional</u>, as used in this passage means

☐ a. old.

☐ b. standard.

☐ c. expensive.

☐ d. unusual.

_____

Add your scores for questions 1-6. Enter the total here and on the graph on page 237.

Total Score ☐

123

51

Talking with Dolphins

Of all the creatures on earth, dolphins seem the most likely to learn to talk with human beings. In relation to their size, their brains are as large as a human's. Like humans, they are mammals. They wander over all the oceans, much as people make their homes in many places on the land. Most importantly, dolphins have a tight social system, and seem to be able to speak to each other very well.

People have tried to talk with dolphins in a number of different ways. Some people have tried to learn dolphin speech. But it consists of whistles, clicks, and creaks that are hard for a human voice to repeat. Dolphins seem to have an easier time imitating human speech. When their sounds are recorded and played back at a slower speed, distinct human words can sometimes be heard. But dolphins usually talk to each other at fast speeds, and use sounds even higher than the human ear can hear. The most promising dolphin communication tool is a machine that can make dolphin sounds. Simple sounds that a dolphin makes for "left," "right," "fish," and "ball" are tape recorded. Each of these sounds can be played back at the press of a button. Whole sentences of speech can be made by combining different sounds. Some day, long <u>discourses</u> between dolphins and people might be held.

		Answer	Score
Main Idea	1		
	Mark the *main idea* ————→	**M**	15
	Mark the statement that is *too broad* ———→	**B**	5
	Mark the statement that is *too narrow* ———→	**N**	5

a. Dolphins are sociable, intelligent creatures. ☐ ———

b. Dolphins are the animals most likely to be able to communicate with people. ☐ ———

c. Dolphins communicate with each other very well. ☐ ———

Score 15 points for each correct answer.   **Score**

Subject Matter

2 Another good title for this passage is
- ☐ a. The Structure of Languages.
- ☐ b. Learning and Society.
- ☐ c. Communicating with Dolphins.
- ☐ d. Underwater Adventures.   _____

Supporting Details

3 Dolphins speak
- ☐ a. in long, complicated sentences.
- ☐ b. with very simple sounds.
- ☐ c. very much like humans.
- ☐ d. very quickly, in whistles, clicks and creaks.   _____

Conclusion

4 From this passage we can conclude that dolphins
- ☐ a. prefer to be alone.
- ☐ b. like people.
- ☐ c. like tape recorders.
- ☐ d. don't communicate well.   _____

Clarifying Devices

5 "People have tried to talk with dolphins in a number of different ways" introduces a paragraph of
- ☐ a. different communication methods that have been tried.
- ☐ b. questions about dolphin speech.
- ☐ c. facts about dolphins.
- ☐ d. reasons why people can't communicate with dolphins.   _____

Vocabulary in Context

6 A <u>discourse</u> is a
- ☐ a. machine.
- ☐ b. conversation.
- ☐ c. test.
- ☐ d. race.   _____

Add your scores for questions 1-6. Enter the total here and on the graph on page 237.   **Total Score** ☐

52

The Knacker

It takes a certain knack to be a knacker. In the days before cars were common, a person called a knacker hauled away horses that had died on the city streets. He took the old <u>plugs</u> to a glue factory where he sold them for profit.

Jack Brennock was Chicago's best-known knacker. Although Jack hauled horses from the streets, he found that he could make more money buying directly from the firemen. When a firehorse died, Jack Brennock was right there to pick it up. He soon became a rich man, buying horses for a dollar and selling them to factories for five.

Perhaps it was greed that caused Jack Brennock to make a costly error. One day Old Danny Boy passed away. He had been the firemen's favorite horse. As usual, Jack came by and whisked the dead animal away. The firemen had planned a funeral for Danny Boy. But before they knew it, their favorite horse was at a glue factory. They were so angry with Jack that they put a curse on him.

In the meantime, Jack had made a decision. He had decided to stop hauling dead horses and start racing live ones. Making money at the races was not as easy as he had expected. Jack's horses lost more races than they won, and in a short time he was broke. Penniless, Jack died in the streets, just like the dead horses who'd made his fortune for him. Some blame Jack's downfall on the firemen's curse. But it might be argued that Jack's biggest curse was greed.

Main Idea	1		Answer	Score
		Mark the *main idea* ⟶	M	15
		Mark the statement that is *too broad* ⟶	B	5
		Mark the statement that is *too narrow* ⟶	N	5

a. Rich men have sometimes become poor very quickly. ☐ ____

b. Jack Brennock made money as a knacker but lost it racing horses. ☐ ____

c. Jack became poor when his race horses kept losing. ☐ ____

Subject Matter   **2**   This passage is about

☐ a. Jack Brennock.

☐ b. Danny Boy.

☐ c. firemen.

☐ d. glue making.   _____

Supporting Details   **3**   Jack bought dead horses for one dollar and sold them for

☐ a. live horses.

☐ b. a fire truck.

☐ c. five dollars.

☐ d. meat.   _____

Conclusion   **4**   The writer of the passage seems to think that Jack's main problem was

☐ a. stupidity.

☐ b. witchcraft.

☐ c. greed.

☐ d. old age.   _____

Clarifying Devices   **5**   To say that Old Danny Boy "passed away" means that he

☐ a. went to another fire company.

☐ b. passed out of sight.

☐ c. died.

☐ d. walked past the knacker.   _____

Vocabulary in Context   **6**   An old <u>plug</u> is a

☐ a. promotional gimmick.

☐ b. worn-out horse.

☐ c. fire hydrant.

☐ d. device at the end of an electrical cord.   _____

Add your scores for questions 1-6. Enter the total here and on the graph on page 237.

Total Score ☐

53

Feeling the Forecast

To find out what the weather is going to be, most people go straight to the radio, television or newspaper to get an expert weather forecast. But if you know what to look for, you can use your own senses to make weather predictions.

There are many signs which can help you. For example, in fair weather the air pressure is generally high. The air is still and often full of dust. Faraway objects may look hazy. But when a storm is brewing, the pressure drops and you are often able to see things more clearly. Sailors took note of this long ago and came up with a saying "The farther the sight, the nearer the rain."

Your sense of smell can also help you detect weather changes. Just before it rains, odors become stronger. This is because odors are repressed in a fair, high-pressure center. When a bad weather low moves in, air pressure lessens and odors are released.

You can also hear an approaching storm. Sounds bounce off heavy storm clouds and return to earth with increased force. An old saying describes it this way: "Sound traveling far and wide, a stormy day will betide."

And don't scoff if your grandmother says she can feel a storm coming. It is commonly known that many people feel pains in their bones or in corns and bunions when the humidity rises, the pressure drops, and bad weather is on the way.

Main Idea	1		Answer	Score
	Mark the *main idea* ⟶	M		15
	Mark the statement that is *too broad* ⟶	B		5
	Mark the statement that is *too narrow* ⟶	N		5

a. You can use your senses to detect weather changes. ☐ _____

b. Seeing and hearing approaching storms is possible. ☐ _____

c. With a little training, we can use our senses more effectively. ☐ _____

Subject Matter   **2**   The topic of this passage is

☐   a. expert weather forecasters.
☐   b. seeing approaching storms.
☐   c. old sayings about weather.
☐   d. using the senses to detect weather changes.   _____

Supporting Details   **3**   According to the passage, as a storm approaches, faraway objects look

☐   a. hazy because of dust in the air.
☐   b. clearer because air pressure is high.
☐   c. clearer because air pressure is dropping.
☐   d. distorted because of storm clouds.   _____

Conclusion   **4**   In the last paragraph, the writer implies that

☐   a. the idea of feeling a coming storm is foolish.
☐   b. older people know a lot about weather.
☐   c. it is possible, but unlikely, that people feel aches when a storm is coming.
☐   d. it is definitely true that some people can feel coming weather changes.   _____

Clarifying Devices   **5**   The writer quotes the old saying "The farther the sight, the nearer the rain" in order to

☐   a. show how foolish and untrue such sayings were.
☐   b. show that this observation, made long ago, is true.
☐   c. convince the reader that expert predictions are not reliable.
☐   d. give the reader a visual image.   _____

Vocabulary in Context   **6**   As used in this passage, <u>repressed</u> is closest in meaning to

☐   a. spread out.
☐   b. composed.
☐   c. trapped.
☐   d. hidden.   _____

Add your scores for questions 1-6. Enter the total here and on the graph on page 237.   Total Score ☐

54

The Ancient Cockroach

He was there to greet the dinosaurs when they arrived on earth. He is still with us 170 million years and billions of kitchens later. Rather than being honored, this <u>sage</u> is despised. Nobody likes a cockroach. Perhaps our hatred of this hearty insect is due to envy. No creature knows more about survival than the cockroach. He can live in the middle of the desert or under a kitchen sink. Lately, roaches have even been found living in TV sets—the parts that heat up provide warmth, and the wax in the set serves as food. Roaches can survive on almost anything from rose petals to laundry soap. They can even do without any food or water at all for up to a month.

Cockroaches like living with people because there's always food around. Even ships at sea are plagued by cockroaches. One sea captain offered a bottle of brandy to any sailor who could catch one thousand roaches on board the ship. The crew turned in 32,000 of the pests. Many fancy poisons are used to kill roaches, but there is no hope of getting rid of them completely. The roach's existence is a creepy fact of life on earth.

Main Idea   1

	Answer	Score
Mark the *main idea* ⟶	**M**	15
Mark the statement that is *too broad* ⟶	**B**	5
Mark the statement that is *too narrow* ⟶	**N**	5

a. The cockroach is one of the world's great survivors. ☐ _____

b. The cockroach can eat almost anything. ☐ _____

c. It's amazing that some creatures have survived on earth for millions of years. ☐ _____

Subject Matter   **2** Another good title for this passage would be

    ☐ a. How Cockroaches Eat.

    ☐ b. The Hearty Cockroach.

    ☐ c. Pest Control.

    ☐ d. Brandy Reward.   _____

Supporting Details   **3** Cockroaches that live in television sets eat

    ☐ a. laundry soap.

    ☐ b. rose petals.

    ☐ c. dust.

    ☐ d. wax.   _____

Conclusion   **4** The first sentence of the passage suggests that

    ☐ a. dinosaurs are older than cockroaches.

    ☐ b. there was only one cockroach 170 million years ago.

    ☐ c. cockroaches existed before dinosaurs.

    ☐ d. cockroaches helped to kill off the dinosaurs.   _____

Clarifying Devices   **5** The author makes the point that cockroaches can survive anywhere by using

    ☐ a. detailed word pictures.

    ☐ b. scientific studies.

    ☐ c. several different facts.

    ☐ d. horror stories.   _____

Vocabulary in Context   **6** A sage is

    ☐ a. an herb.

    ☐ b. someone old and wise.

    ☐ c. a western bush.

    ☐ d. a story.   _____

Add your scores for questions 1-6. Enter the total here and on the graph on page 237.   Total Score [   ]

55

Famous Horses of the Past

Did you think only kings and queens lived in marble houses? Well Caligula, a Roman Emperor, kept his horse, Incitatus, in a marble stable! The horse's stall was made of ivory. He wore a golden collar inlaid with jewels. His purple blanket was a sign of royalty. It was rumored that Caligula had even made his horse consul! A consul was a ruler with much power.

Horses have helped to shape history. Long ago, winning or losing a battle often depended on how fast a horse could run. Horses were crucial in war. General Robert E. Lee never parted with Traveller, his horse. During the American Civil War, General Lee led the Confederate Army. Traveller braved many battles with Lee, and was never hurt.

The most famous war horse of all time was made of wood! It actually helped defeat an entire army. About thirty-five hundred years ago, a fierce battle was going on between the Trojans and the ancient Greeks in a place called Asia Minor. The Greeks tried to think of a way to outsmart their enemies. At last, they built a huge wooden horse, taller than two houses, and left it outside the gates of the city of Troy. Since they didn't know where it came from, the Trojans thought the horse had magical powers. Carefully, they pulled it through the gates. That night, a surprising thing happened. The sides of the wooden horse opened and a band of Greek soldiers climbed out. They opened the gates of Troy and let in the Greek army. The Greeks soon captured the city of Troy.

Main Idea 1

	Answer	Score
Mark the *main idea* ⟶	M	15
Mark the statement that is *too broad* ⟶	B	5
Mark the statement that is *too narrow* ⟶	N	5

a. Horses are interesting animals. ☐ ____

b. Horses helped to shape history. ☐ ____

c. The most famous war horse was the Trojan horse. ☐ ____

Subject Matter

2 The subject matter of this passage is

☐ a. horses in history.

☐ b. horses of war.

☐ c. magical powers.

☐ d. Greek soldiers.   _____

Supporting Details

3 According to this passage, the Trojan horse

☐ a. had magical powers.

☐ b. was made of wood.

☐ c. led thousands of soldiers.

☐ d. was never wounded.   _____

Conclusion

4 The Trojans did <u>not</u> expect to find

☐ a. soldiers inside the horse.

☐ b. weapons inside the horse.

☐ c. such a wonderful gift.

☐ d. that the gods favored them.   _____

Clarifying Devices

5 The first sentence in the second paragraph tells what

☐ a. the author wants most to tell us in this passage.

☐ b. horses are usually raised for.

☐ c. can be done by an intelligent horse.

☐ d. must be done to train a war horse.   _____

Vocabulary in Context

6 If something is <u>crucial</u>, it is

☐ a. needed very much.

☐ b. difficult to understand.

☐ c. very fast.

☐ d. surprising.   _____

Add your scores for questions 1-6. Enter the total here and on the graph on page 237.

Total Score ☐

56

Insects Could Take Over

Is that a worm in your apple? Folks who shop at the supermarket rarely have to worry about finding a worm in their apple, or even sharing their tomato with a beetle. This is only because the farmers who grow the food fight a constant war against insects. Yet, even with scores of potent poisons to use as weapons, it is a war that is never really won.

There are many reasons why you can't get rid of all insect pests. One is that there are so many bugs. The world is full of crawling creatures. A spray that kills one kind of bug may just make another kind queasy. And only a few different chemicals can be sprayed on any one crop. If a very general chemical is used, it can make things worse. It may hurt the creatures that eat the pests more than it hurts the pests themselves! The result: more pests than before the chemical was used. Using very strong chemicals can harm the plants and the people who eat them more than they harm the insects.

Luckily, not all the insects on a crop have to be killed. A few chemicals used at the right time usually keep the number of bugs low enough that most of the plants will be healthy and pest-free. These healthy crops are the apples and tomatoes we find in the stores. Most people don't realize how hard it was to save them from the insects.

Main Idea	1		Answer	Score
	Mark the *main idea* ⟶	M		15
	Mark the statement that is *too broad* ⟶	B		5
	Mark the statement that is *too narrow* ⟶	N		5
	a. Farmers use chemicals to kill insects.	☐		___
	b. A constant war must be fought against insect pests on food crops.	☐		___
	c. Insects are both harmful and helpful to mankind.	☐		___

Subject Matter

2 This passage is mostly about

☐ a. the farmers' war against insects.

☐ b. insect pests found in supermarkets.

☐ c. the danger of eating poisoned apples.

☐ d. why chemicals are harmful.   _____

Supporting Details

3 According to this passage, what kind of chemical is dangerous to people?

☐ a. A very general one

☐ b. A long-lasting one

☐ c. A very strong one

☐ d. A widely used one   _____

Conclusion

4 A chemical that kills the creatures that eat harmful insects probably

☐ a. is most helpful to a farmer.

☐ b. is dangerous to people too.

☐ c. does more harm than good.

☐ d. has little effect on the plants.   _____

Clarifying Devices

5 The author compares the farmers' fight against insects to

☐ a. a contest.

☐ b. a war.

☐ c. a game.

☐ d. a puzzle.   _____

Vocabulary in Context

6 A potent poison is one that

☐ a. smells terrible.

☐ b. is manmade.

☐ c. comes as a liquid.

☐ d. is very powerful.   _____

Add your scores for questions 1–6. Enter the total here and on the graph on page 237.

Total Score ☐

57

Without Hook and Line

The people of the Maori tribe of New Zealand take their tickling seriously. Their survival depends on their ability to tickle. Tickling might not sound like a very hard or useful activity. But for the Maori, tickling is an important way to get food. The Maori practice their own brand of tickling on fish.

There are many fish in the shallow coastal waters of New Zealand. They are a main staple in the diet of the Maori. To catch the fish, a fisherman must first walk slowly and quietly in the shallow water. But the fish are wary. They often hide near jagged rocks and coral reefs. They swim quickly from one hiding place to another. But sometimes the hiding fish will sleep. This is when they are most <u>vulnerable</u> to the Maori's entrancing tickle.

When he spots a sleeping fish, the keen-eyed fisherman is set to make his move. Very slowly and cautiously he bends down and starts to tickle his napping food. The sleeping fish responds to the tickle by wiggling from its hiding spot. With a quick movement, the Maori fisherman reaches for the stunned fish. He holds on as tightly as he can with both hands. Supper has been caught with a tickle. The Maori's fishing techniques may be unusual, but they have been successful for many centuries.

		Answer	Score
Main Idea	1		
	Mark the *main idea* ⟶	M	15
	Mark the statement that is *too broad* ⟶	B	5
	Mark the statement that is *too narrow* ⟶	N	5

a. The Maori have unusual methods of gathering food. ☐ _____

b. It is easy to tickle fish when they are sleeping. ☐ _____

c. The Maori catch fish by tickling them. ☐ _____

Score 15 points for each correct answer.

Subject Matter **2** Another good title for this passage would be
- ☐ a. The Maori Comedians.
- ☐ b. Fishing in New Zealand.
- ☐ c. The Tickling Tribe of New Zealand.
- ☐ d. Funny Fish.   _____

Supporting Details **3** The Maori catch their fish in the shallow waters of
- ☐ a. the lakes.
- ☐ b. a stream.
- ☐ c. the coast.
- ☐ d. a swamp.   _____

Conclusion **4** This passage might best be summed up by saying that
- ☐ a. the Maori are a curious tribe.
- ☐ b. the Maori are among the bravest people in the world.
- ☐ c. tickling fish is a valuable Maori skill.
- ☐ d. tickling fish is an exciting Maori sport.   _____

Clarifying Devices **5** The writer begins this passage by
- ☐ a. saying surprising things about tickling.
- ☐ b. telling a funny story.
- ☐ c. answering questions about tickling.
- ☐ d. describing the Maori tribe of New Zealand.   _____

Vocabulary in Context **6** <u>Vulnerable</u> means
- ☐ a. afraid of.
- ☐ b. surprised by.
- ☐ c. open to attack.
- ☐ d. ticklish.   _____

Add your scores for questions 1-6. Enter the total here and on the graph on page 237.   **Total Score** ☐

58

The Ship with Four Legs

Only one animal can walk 200 miles without stopping once to rest. It would take a person two days and two nights to walk this far, and only one man has ever done it without stopping. What amazing animal has such endurance? The camel! The camel is well known for something else, too. It can cross an entire desert without a single drink of water. Its body is built in a special way to help it store water and food.

A person has just one stomach, but a camel has quite a few. Within each stomach are layers and layers of cells. These cells are like tiny water balloons, storing liquids until the camel needs them. When the camel drinks, the cells grow larger and larger. For a whole week, they can keep the animal's thirst away by sending water to all parts of its body.

And did you ever wonder why the camel has a hump? The hump is a storage place for fat. Because it has this storage area, the camel does not need to eat very often. When the animal needs energy, the layers of fat serve as fuel to keep it going on the long, hot days in the burning sun.

The camel has one other gift that makes it well suited to arid regions. This gift is its amazing nose. A camel can smell a water hole from miles away!

When a camel moves it sways from side to side like a ship on a wavy ocean. Because of this swaying motion, the camel has been called the "Ship of the Desert."

Main Idea	1		Answer	Score
		Mark the *main idea* ———→	M	15
		Mark the statement that is *too broad* ——→	B	5
		Mark the statement that is *too narrow* ——→	N	5

a. Desert animals have great endurance. ☐ _____

b. Camels can store liquids in their bodies for long periods. ☐ _____

c. The camel is built to survive in the desert. ☐ _____

Score 15 points for each correct answer.

Subject Matter   **2**   This passage is mainly about
- ☐ a. long-distance walking.
- ☐ b. mysterious ships.
- ☐ c. the camel.
- ☐ d. desert animals.

_____

Supporting Details   **3**   The camel's hump is a storage place for
- ☐ a. muscles.
- ☐ b. extra water.
- ☐ c. body sugars.
- ☐ d. fat.

_____

Conclusion   **4**   We can conclude from this passage that camels
- ☐ a. feel at home in the desert.
- ☐ b. like to carry heavy loads.
- ☐ c. look like ships from a distance.
- ☐ d. will always be useful.

_____

Clarifying Devices   **5**   The author compares cells with water balloons in order to
- ☐ a. make you think of summer.
- ☐ b. help you visualize the cells.
- ☐ c. show how rubber is elastic.
- ☐ d. show how many shapes cells can have.

_____

Vocabulary in Context   **6**   The word arid is closest in meaning to
- ☐ a. sunny.
- ☐ b. flat.
- ☐ c. dry.
- ☐ d. sandy.

_____

Add your scores for questions 1–6. Enter the total here and on the graph on page 237.

Total Score ☐

59

Knock! Knock!

Knock on wood. Woodpeckers do just that. This bird is an amazing creature. It pecks so hard and fast that its head looks like a blur. The woodpecker knocks on dead wood, looking for insects to eat. Its chisel-like beak chips away bark and decayed wood. The violent tapping disturbs insects hidden in the tree's cavities. When the woodpecker reaches the insects' home, it spears its dinner with a barbed and sticky tongue.

The woodpecker pecks at a speed of 1300 miles per hour. At this speed, the impact of the bird's beak hitting the wood is almost like that of a supersonic jet smashing into a mountain. Each peck takes just a thousandth of a second. The movement is quicker than the human eye can follow. Incredibly, the bird's cherry-sized brain is never injured from all this furious smashing.

There is a secret to the woodpecker's ability to withstand, without injury, the great impact of its pecking. The secret lies in the woodpecker's neck muscles. They are so well coordinated that the head and beak move only in a straight line. This spreads the shock evenly through the bird's body and into the tree trunk. Pecking at even a slight angle would kill the woodpecker. Design experts are using this bird as a model. They hope to come up with a crash helmet that will better protect people's heads from injuries.

Main Idea   1

	Answer	Score
Mark the *main idea* ⟶	M	15
Mark the statement that is *too broad* ⟶	B	5
Mark the statement that is *too narrow* ⟶	N	5

a. The woodpecker is specially built to survive the great shock of its hard, fast pecking. ☐ _____

b. Birds are specially adapted to their habitats and way of life. ☐ _____

c. The impact of a woodpecker's pecking is very great. ☐ _____

Subject Matter   **2**   The subject of this passage is

☐ a. knocking on wood.
☐ b. woodpeckers.
☐ c. whiplash.
☐ d. designing crash helmets.   _____

Supporting Details   **3**   The woodpecker doesn't get injured while pecking because it

☐ a. has a small brain.
☐ b. has specially adapted neck muscles.
☐ c. knocks only on dead wood.
☐ d. pecks faster than the eye can follow.   _____

Conclusion   **4**   The writer concludes that

☐ a. woodpeckers are well liked.
☐ b. people are annoyed by the tapping noise of woodpeckers.
☐ c. scientists can benefit from the study of woodpeckers.
☐ d. woodpeckers are important to the ecology of the forest.   _____

Clarifying Devices   **5**   The writer tries to demonstrate the great impact of a peck with

☐ a. a comparison.
☐ b. a story.
☐ c. an example.
☐ d. a definition.   _____

Vocabulary in Context   **6**   Furious pecking is

☐ a. angry.
☐ b. needless.
☐ c. unbearable.
☐ d. violent.   _____

Add your scores for questions 1-6. Enter the total here and on the graph on page 237.   Total Score ☐

60

The Spider Cloud

The appearance of dark rain clouds on a sunny day is bad enough. Can you image what it would be like if clouds filled with spiders drifted in? Well, people in St. Louis, Missouri, were treated to this weird weather.

At first the drifting cloud looked like a dense fog. But it was filled with strange dark spots. Workers at McDonnell-Douglas Space Center began to investigate it. Were these fragments of a spaceship that had burned up before it could reach earth? Were they tiny <u>cells</u> from another planet? Even after looking at the cloud with a strong telescope, the experts were stumped. Finally, biologists were able to get some of the globules from the cloud. They were made of weblike fibers. The scientists unwound the fibers like a spool of thread. To their surprise, they found spiders.

The spider cloud turned out to be a normal part of the spiders' natural reproductive process. It was filled with baby balloon spiders. The female balloon spider has a strange way of protecting her young. When it comes time to lay her eggs, she climbs to the top of a tall tree. It's hard work, almost like climbing a skyscraper would be for us. At the top of the tree, the female spider spins her web and deposits her eggs in it. Then she cuts the fibers of the web as one would cut the strings of a bunch of balloons. The tiny spiders float away to unknown homes.

Main Idea	1		Answer	Score
		Mark the *main idea*	M	15
		Mark the statement that is *too broad*	B	5
		Mark the statement that is *too narrow*	N	5

a. The balloon spider protects her babies by sending them off in a web that floats in the air. ☐ ____

b. Spiders have unusual ways of protecting their young. ☐ ____

c. Baby balloon spiders drift through the air in a floating web. ☐ ____

Score 15 points for each correct answer.   **Score**

Subject Matter   **2** This passage is about

☐ a. unusually tall trees.
☐ b. balloon spiders.
☐ c. biologists.
☐ d. unidentified flying objects.   _____

Supporting Details   **3** The tiny balloon spiders are wrapped in a

☐ a. spool of yarn.
☐ b. cocoon.
☐ c. web of fibers.
☐ d. balloon.   _____

Conclusion   **4** We may conclude that

☐ a. people in Missouri have unusual weather.
☐ b. balloon spiders live in high trees.
☐ c. balloon spiders have an unusual reproductive cycle.
☐ d. biologists study only spiders.   _____

Clarifying Devices   **5** In the last paragraph, the writer helps you imagine how hard the female spider works by

☐ a. comparing the spider's efforts to human efforts.
☐ b. describing the tall trees.
☐ c. giving detailed facts.
☐ d. describing how balloon strings are cut.   _____

Vocabulary in Context   **6** The word <u>cells</u>, as used in this passage, means

☐ a. rooms in a jail.
☐ b. a small group within a larger organization.
☐ c. the building blocks for plants and animals.
☐ d. spaceships.   _____

Add your scores for questions 1-6. Enter the total here and on the graph on page 237.   **Total Score** ☐

143

61

Mix-up in the Sky

Do you know the order of the planets? The planet closest to the sun is fiery Mercury. Next comes hot and humid Venus, followed by the green Earth. Fourth in line is red and dusty Mars. The fifth planet from the sun is the giant Jupiter. Then comes ringed Saturn, mysterious Uranus, misty Neptune, and, finally, cold and lonely Pluto. Right?

Wrong! The planet Pluto has temporarily moved in closer to the sun than Neptune. Pluto is now the eighth planet, and Neptune the ninth. For nineteen years, until the year 2000, Neptune will be the farthest planet from the sun.

This strange mix-up is due to the orbits of the planets around the sun. Many people think the planets move in circles. Actually, they move in oval-shaped patterns called "ellipses." Most planets have orbits that are quite regular. Pluto's orbit, however, is extremely <u>eccentric</u> when compared to the other planets. Every 284 years, its irregular orbit brings it closer to the sun, moving it into place as the eighth planet, rather than the ninth. Because Pluto is so small, some astronomers think it was once a satellite of Neptune that was knocked into its strange orbit by some ancient cosmic catastrophe.

Main Idea   1

	Answer	Score
Mark the *main idea* ⟶	M	15
Mark the statement that is *too broad* ⟶	B	5
Mark the statement that is *too narrow* ⟶	N	5

a. The planets have changed their positions. ☐ ____

b. Pluto is now the eighth planet. ☐ ____

c. Pluto has a very strange orbit. ☐ ____

**Subject
Matter**

2 This passage is mostly about the planets

☐ a. Pluto and Uranus.

☐ b. Neptune and Pluto.

☐ c. Earth and Venus.

☐ d. Uranus and Mercury.   _____

**Supporting
Details**

3 Pluto's orbit is different because of

☐ a. the small size of the planet.

☐ b. an ancient accident in space.

☐ c. its distance from the sun.

☐ d. the coldness of space.   _____

Conclusion

4 We can assume from the passage that Pluto

☐ a. will move closer and closer to the sun.

☐ b. was once a larger planet.

☐ c. will be the ninth planet again in the
year 2000.

☐ d. is not cold anymore.   _____

**Clarifying
Devices**

5 The phrase "due to" means

☐ a. because of.

☐ b. from which.

☐ c. in spite of.

☐ d. in case of.   _____

**Vocabulary
in Context**

6 The word <u>eccentric,</u> as used in this
passage, means

☐ a. old.

☐ b. strange.

☐ c. circular.

☐ d. egg-shaped.   _____

**Add your scores for questions 1-6. Enter the
total here and on the graph on page 238.**

**Total
Score** ☐

62

Seeing Yourself Successful

"They laughed when I sat down at the piano, but when I started to play . . . !" These words may be among the most successful in advertising history. Although the ad has not run for many years, the slogan is still remembered. It was written in 1925 for the U.S. School of Music, to sell home music lessons.

The ad has great appeal. It pictures a handsome man sitting at a piano in front of smiling guests. It tells the story of Jack, who has secretly learned to play the piano through a mail-order course. His friends at a party all scoff when he sits at the keyboard. But as he plays the first notes of Beethoven's "Moonlight Sonata," they are amazed. When he finishes his flawless performance, the listeners shower him with applause and praise.

Jack tells his friends that he learned to play through the U.S. School of Music. He explains that he was taught through a new method, using no laborious scales and no tiresome practicing. He didn't even have a special talent for music! In the ad, others were urged to send in a coupon so they, too, could increase their popularity and gain happiness.

The writer of this ad, John Caples, called this style the "Walter Mitty approach." Walter Mitty is a character in a short story by James Thurber, who daydreams of taking part in great adventures. Although this ad seems old-fashioned now, many people still dream of such easy social success.

Main Idea	1	Answer	Score
Mark the *main idea* ⟶		M	15
Mark the statement that is *too broad* ⟶		B	5
Mark the statement that is *too narrow* ⟶		N	5
a. Mail-order courses promise great opportunities.		☐	_____
b. A successful U.S. School of Music ad appealed to people's dreams of social success.		☐	_____
c. The U.S. School of Music had a course that taught people to play the piano.		☐	_____

Score 15 points for each correct answer. **Score**

Subject Matter

2 This passage is about a
- [ ] a. musical performance.
- [ ] b. successful advertisement.
- [ ] c. valuable prize.
- [ ] d. scientific study.

_____

Supporting Details

3 Walter Mitty is
- [ ] a. a successful ad man.
- [ ] b. a short-story writer.
- [ ] c. a beginning piano player.
- [ ] d. a fictional character.

_____

Conclusion

4 The author of this passage implies that nowadays the story of Jack would be
- [ ] a. believable.
- [ ] b. inspiring.
- [ ] c. unbelievable.
- [ ] d. sad.

_____

Clarifying Devices

5 The opening sentence catches your attention by
- [ ] a. surprising you.
- [ ] b. describing a humorous situation.
- [ ] c. ridiculing someone.
- [ ] d. appealing to people's dreams of personal success.

_____

Vocabulary in Context

6 An action that is <u>laborious</u> is
- [ ] a. humorous.
- [ ] b. difficult.
- [ ] c. effortless.
- [ ] d. swift.

_____

Add your scores for questions 1-6. Enter the total here and on the graph on page 238.

Total Score [   ]

63

The Monstrous Flower

Have you ever heard of a flower whose seeds are carried and spread by elephants? The rafflesia, a rare blossom, is very unusual. Found in the rain forests of Sumatra, the rafflesia is the world's largest flower, measuring three feet in diameter!

This giant flower is a parasite—it needs another plant to live on. It lacks the <u>structures</u> needed to survive alone. The rafflesia has no stem or leaves. It is all flower. It attaches itself to the roots of other plants and sucks their juices. The flower's favorite home is the root of the cissus vine, which grows above ground.

The rafflesia seems to burst right out of the forest floor. Its blossom weighs fifteen pounds! It has thick, spotted petals that give off a foul smell. The center, or nectary, is about the size of a household bucket. After a rain, it may hold up to twelve pints of water!

After the rafflesia dies, it becomes a pool of thick liquid in which its seeds float. Elephants wandering through the forest step into the mushy pool, and the seeds glue themselves to their feet. As the animals stomp through the forest, their sticky feet pick up twigs and leaves. The elephants try to rid themselves of the sticky mess, in the same way people try to get bubble gum off their shoes. The elephants rub their feet against the roots of the cissus vine. In no time, seeds left on the vine grow into more monstrous flowers!

Main Idea	1		Answer	Score
		Mark the *main idea* ⟶	M	15
		Mark the statement that is *too broad* ⟶	B	5
		Mark the statement that is *too narrow* ⟶	N	5

a. The rafflesia is one of the world's most unusual flowers. ☐ _____

b. Some flowers grow in strange ways. ☐ _____

c. The rafflesia has no root structure of its own. ☐ _____

Score 15 points for each correct answer.   **Score**

Subject Matter

2 This passage is about

☐ a. wandering elephants.

☐ b. the rafflesia.

☐ c. cissus vines.

☐ d. parasites.   _____

Supporting Details

3 Elephants help to

☐ a. provide food for the giant flower.

☐ b. water the rafflesia with their trunks.

☐ c. carry rafflesia seeds from one place to another.

☐ d. stomp out the awful smelling petals.   _____

Conclusion

4 From this passage, we can guess that the writer

☐ a. likes elephants.

☐ b. has a very large garden.

☐ c. admires the wonders of nature.

☐ d. likes to measure things.   _____

Clarifying Devices

5 To give us an idea of how large the rafflesia is, the author uses

☐ a. the size of an elephant for comparison.

☐ b. measurements.

☐ c. comparisons to other flowers.

☐ d. detailed descriptions of the flower's stem.   _____

Vocabulary in Context

6 As used in this passage, <u>structures</u> means

☐ a. endurance.

☐ b. organization.

☐ c. necessary parts.

☐ d. energy.   _____

Add your scores for questions 1-6. Enter the total here and on the graph on page 238.

Total Score ☐

64

Boat Ride to the Center of the Earth

A group of scientists rowing toward the center of a lake saw something shocking. They turned back as fast as they could. What had they seen? The lake was boiling!

The group was investigating a crater lake in the mountains of St. Vincent, an island in the Caribbean. A crater lake is the mouth of a volcano that has been <u>dormant</u> for some time and has filled with water.

This particular crater was the tip of a volcano called Soufriere, which erupted last in 1902. Since that time, it had not shown any signs of action. But in the fall of 1971, mountain climbers who had hiked near the lake returned to the lowlands with strange stories. They said the water had turned yellow and was giving off a smell like burnt eggs. A seething fog was rising from the lake's surface.

Local scientists rushed to Soufriere to see if this might be the beginning of a new volcanic explosion. They found a huge black mass in the middle of the water. It was a great blob 1,000 feet long and 300 feet wide. Lava had pushed up through the bottom of the lake and formed a new island.

The investigators wanted to make sure that the volcano was safe, and that the lava would not overflow into the surrounding countryside. But they could never reach the island to study it, because the lava was so hot that the water around it bubbled and boiled.

Main Idea	1		Answer	Score
	Mark the *main idea* ⟶	**M**		15
	Mark the statement that is *too broad* ⟶	**B**		5
	Mark the statement that is *too narrow* ⟶	**N**		5
	a. A new island, made of lava, formed in a crater lake in Mount Soufriere.	☐		____
	b. The molten rock within the earth is powerful and dangerous.	☐		____
	c. The water in the crater lake on Soufriere bubbled and boiled.	☐		____

Score 15 points for each correct answer.   Score

Subject   **2** This passage is about
Matter
    ☐ a. mountain climbing.
    ☐ b. a boiling lake.
    ☐ c. a new volcanic island.
    ☐ d. a mysterious blob.   _____

Supporting **3** A crater lake is at the tip of a
Details
    ☐ a. mountain.
    ☐ b. ridge.
    ☐ c. island.
    ☐ d. volcano.   _____

Conclusion **4** We can conclude that
    ☐ a. the situation was nothing to be
        concerned about.
    ☐ b. Soufriere is still an active volcano.
    ☐ c. crater lakes are easy to hike to.
    ☐ d. Soufriere is a dead volcano.   _____

Clarifying **5** The writer explains the boiling water by using
Devices
    ☐ a. myths.
    ☐ b. humor.
    ☐ c. facts.
    ☐ d. arguments.   _____

Vocabulary **6** Another word for dormant might be
in Context
    ☐ a. muddy.
    ☐ b. boiling.
    ☐ c. inactive.
    ☐ d. threatening.   _____

Add your scores for questions 1-6. Enter the   **Total** ☐
total here and on the graph on page 238.   **Score**

65

The World of Dieting

Americans are well known for the strange diets they always seem to be following. It seems that Americans like to diet almost as much as they like to eat. New types of diet plans are always coming out. Usually, though, they don't stay popular for long.

There are many diets on the market. It is often difficult to know which ones really work. It's also hard to believe how fast a dieter is supposed to shed pounds. A lot has been written about dieting. And some interesting facts about diets and foods have been discovered.

For example, did you know that the more celery you eat, the more weight you will lose? Celery has "negative" calories. The body burns up more calories digesting a piece of celery than there are in the celery stick itself.

Dieters <u>shun</u> potatoes because they think they are fattening. But they aren't. A potato has about the same number of calories as an apple. To gain a single pound, you would have to eat eleven pounds of potatoes!

Some dieters even worry about getting fat from licking postage stamps. But they have nothing to worry about. The glue on an average stamp has only about one-tenth of a calorie. Maybe a diet of postage stamps would be popular?

Main Idea	1		Answer	Score
		Mark the *main idea* ⟶	**M**	15
		Mark the statement that is *too broad* ⟶	**B**	5
		Mark the statement that is *too narrow* ⟶	**N**	5

a. Most diets lose their popularity quickly. ☐ ____

b. Some facts about dieting can be surprising. ☐ ____

c. There are many diets on the market. ☐ ____

Score 15 points for each correct answer.   **Score**

Subject Matter

2 This passage is all about
- ☐ a. vegetables.
- ☐ b. fads.
- ☐ c. Americans.
- ☐ d. dieting.   _____

Supporting Details

3 Celery is a good food for the dieter because
- ☐ a. it has a lot of protein.
- ☐ b. vegetables are not fattening.
- ☐ c. it has negative calories.
- ☐ d. it is easy to digest.   _____

Conclusion

4 One could conclude from this passage that
- ☐ a. dieting is not a healthy practice.
- ☐ b. everyone diets.
- ☐ c. there is only one good way to lose weight.
- ☐ d. dieting can be confusing.   _____

Clarifying Devices

5 "On the market" is an expression that means
- ☐ a. being sold.
- ☐ b. in the supermarket.
- ☐ c. prescribed by doctors.
- ☐ d. being talked about.   _____

Vocabulary in Context

6 To <u>shun</u> is to
- ☐ a. love.
- ☐ b. hate.
- ☐ c. avoid.
- ☐ d. fear.   _____

Add your scores for questions 1-6. Enter the total here and on the graph on page 238.

Total Score ☐

66

Protected by Armor

Where can you find a cliff built entirely by animals? On the bottom of the ocean! Underwater reefs are huge walls made by tiny animals called corals. Because corals are very small, reefs take hundreds of years to build.

How do such small animals accomplish such a great task? The reefs are <u>composed</u> of coral skeletons!

The coral animals are called "polyps." They have very soft bodies. Without some kind of "armor," they would be eaten by fish. To protect themselves, they build limestone shells around their bodies.

Coral polyps live in colonies. They connect themselves to each other and to the ocean floor. The corals build their limestone skeletons by taking a mineral called calcium out of the water and depositing it around themselves. The calcium deposits are very hard. As new coral polyps are born and attach themselves to the colony, the formation gets bigger. After a long while, a large reef has grown up.

The largest coral reef is longer than the state of New York. It is the great Barrier Reef of Australia.

Main Idea 1

	Answer	Score
Mark the *main idea* ⟶	**M**	15
Mark the statement that is *too broad* ⟶	**B**	5
Mark the statement that is *too narrow* ⟶	**N**	5

a. Coral reefs are built from the skeletons of tiny ocean animals. ☐ _____

b. Sea creatures create many wonderful things under the surface of the ocean. ☐ _____

c. Coral polyps build their limestone shells from calcium found in the water. ☐ _____

Score 15 points for each correct answer.   **Score**

Subject Matter

2 This passage is mainly about
- ☐ a. limestone.
- ☐ b. Australia.
- ☐ c. coral reefs.
- ☐ d. calcium.   _____

Supporting Details

3 Coral polyps are
- ☐ a. limestone deposits.
- ☐ b. tiny animals.
- ☐ c. minerals.
- ☐ d. long reefs.   _____

Conclusion

4 Coral reefs take a long time to build because
- ☐ a. coral is rare.
- ☐ b. calcium is hard to get.
- ☐ c. corals are tiny.
- ☐ d. the ocean is very deep.   _____

Clarifying Devices

5 The writer helps you to visualize the length of the Great Barrier Reef by
- ☐ a. comparing it to the size of another place.
- ☐ b. describing how long it is.
- ☐ c. telling you its measurements.
- ☐ d. telling you how long it took to build.   _____

Vocabulary in Context

6 The word <u>composed</u> means
- ☐ a. ruined.
- ☐ b. made up of.
- ☐ c. glued together.
- ☐ d. colored by.   _____

Add your scores for questions 1-6. Enter the total here and on the graph on page 238.   **Total Score** ☐

67

What's Going On?

No one likes to travel through the dreaded Bermuda Triangle. Scientists can't explain the strange phenomena that take place there.

The Bermuda Triangle is an area of water in the Atlantic Ocean. The triangle is bounded on its three sides by Bermuda, Florida, and Puerto Rico. For over 200 years, ships, and now planes, have seemed to just disappear there. In 1750 three treasure ships from Spain were lost in this "triangle of fear." No trace of them has ever been found.

The most recent disappearance took place in 1973, when a huge freighter, the *Anita*, was lost along with its entire crew. No one has yet been able to explain what became of the *Anita*.

In 1945 five United States torpedo bombers disappeared in the triangle after taking off from Fort Lauderdale, Florida. The pilots reported that their instruments were "going crazy," just before radio contact with them was lost. A search plane was sent out to look for them. It never returned.

No one really knows why so many ships, planes and human lives have been lost in the Bermuda Triangle. Could it be, as some scientists believe, that storms and downward air currents have destroyed all these ships and planes? Then why have there been no traces of the lost wrecks? Do strong ocean currents carry them all away? Or is it that there really is something strangely evil about this Devil's Triangle?

Main Idea	1		Answer	Score
		Mark the *main idea* ⟶	M	15
		Mark the statement that is *too broad* ⟶	B	5
		Mark the statement that is *too narrow* ⟶	N	5

a. The Bermuda Triangle is one of the strangest places on earth. ☐ ____

b. Scientists can't explain the strange things that happen in the Bermuda Triangle. ☐ ____

c. Ships and planes have often disappeared without a trace in the Bermuda Triangle. ☐ ____

Score 15 points for each correct answer.   **Score**

Subject Matter

2 Another good title for this passage would be
- ☐ a. The Magic of Bermuda.
- ☐ b. Triangle of Fear.
- ☐ c. The Recovery of the *Anita*.
- ☐ d. Solving the Mystery of the Bermuda Triangle.

_____

Supporting Details

3 The last disappearance in the Bermuda Triangle was of
- ☐ a. a freighter called the *Anita*.
- ☐ b. a torpedo bomber.
- ☐ c. three Spanish treasure ships.
- ☐ d. a fishing boat.

_____

Conclusion

4 It is probably true that
- ☐ a. planes and ships avoid the triangle when possible.
- ☐ b. the Bermuda Triangle will grow larger.
- ☐ c. no more planes or ships will disappear in the triangle.
- ☐ d. scientists will soon solve the triangle's mysteries.

_____

Clarifying Devices

5 In the first paragraph, the words "the dreaded Bermuda Triangle" tell us that
- ☐ a. the triangle is unusual.
- ☐ b. people fear the triangle.
- ☐ c. the area of the triangle is stormy.
- ☐ d. people are curious about the triangle.

_____

Vocabulary in Context

6 Phenomena are
- ☐ a. storms.
- ☐ b. disturbances.
- ☐ c. disappearances.
- ☐ d. occurrences.

_____

Add your scores for questions 1-6. Enter the total here and on the graph on page 238.

Total Score ☐

68

The African Elephant

The elephant is the largest of all land animals. It can reach a height of eleven feet and weigh nearly six tons. The African elephant can also boast the biggest ears in the world. They can grow as large as three-and-a-half feet across. You might think that an animal that's so gigantic wouldn't have much to worry about, but it has its problems too. And its huge ears help it to deal with many problems ranging from pesky insects to great danger.

The ears are very effective fans that can be used to swat flies. The elephants' huge ears also help them hear everything that's happening nearby. A mother elephant might hear the approach of a dangerous lion that would kill her calves. Its great size can sometimes be a problem for an elephant. The larger an object, the harder it is for it to lose heat. Elephants live on the hot plains of Africa, where keeping cool is not an easy task. Their huge ears help them cool their bodies so they can survive in the heat. The large surfaces of the ears have many blood vessels that are very close to the surface of the skin. Blood that is closer to the surface cools more easily. The most impressive use of the ears, though, is seen in an elephant's threat display. When trying to threaten another animal, the elephant bellows and charges with both ears spread wide. This makes the huge beast look almost twice as large as it really is. Few enemies would dare to stand up to anything that <u>colossal</u>.

Main Idea	1		Answer	Score
		Mark the *main idea* ———→	M	15
		Mark the statement that is *too broad* ——→	B	5
		Mark the statement that is *too narrow* ——→	N	5

a. Large ears help animals survive. ☐ _____

b. African elephants lose heat through their ears. ☐ _____

c. The huge ears of African elephants help them in many ways. ☐ _____

Score 15 points for each correct answer.   **Score**

Subject Matter

2 Another good title for this passage would be

☐ a. Survival on the African Plains.
☐ b. They're all Ears.
☐ c. Keeping Cool in Africa.
☐ d. The Elephant's Threat Display.   _____

Supporting Details

3 The African elephant's large ears help it to

☐ a. hide.
☐ b. cool off.
☐ c. find food.
☐ d. control its young.   _____

Conclusion

4 We can conclude that if elephants did not have big ears they would probably

☐ a. see better.
☐ b. be smaller.
☐ c. not be able to survive.
☐ d. not live in Africa.   _____

Clarifying Devices

5 The author calls the elephant's threat display "impressive." This means that it is

☐ a. interesting.
☐ b. admirable.
☐ c. frightening.
☐ d. unusual.   _____

Vocabulary in Context

6 Colossal indicates that the elephant appears

☐ a. extremely angry.
☐ b. incredibly large.
☐ c. to be moving very fast.
☐ d. amazingly strong.   _____

Add your scores for questions 1-6. Enter the total here and on the graph on page 238.   **Total Score** ☐

69

Good Idea!

Can a skunk ever be a welcomed guest? For some people it can be. The furry, black-haired animal with the telltale white stripe running down its back can actually be a very friendly pet.

Mrs. Sadie Redekopp of Dallas, Oregon, was one of the first people to think of keeping skunks as pets. One day she spotted four baby skunks peeking out from under her barn, and she was hooked. She found a way to de-scent them, and she kept them as pets.

She had a hunch that other people would like these friendly, adorable animals as pets. She advertised and struck it rich. With baby skunks selling for $10 each, she grossed $80,000 the first year. Mrs. Redekopp's clever idea proved profitable and worthwhile.

Another person who benefited from a creative idea was Cliff Tagere of Boston, Massachusetts. He came up with a use for, of all things, porcupine quills! He glued quills to cards on which he wrote:

> This is a porcupine quill. The porcupine is the best protected animal in the woods. If he ever came to town and saw so many people without insurance, he would laugh himself to death.

Cliff sent the cards to insurance companies as an idea for an advertising gimmick. One big company liked his idea. It asked him to make a quarter of a million of the quill cards. The advertising campaign was a huge success. A creative idea can turn the most common object into a valuable item.

Main Idea	1		Answer	Score
		Mark the *main idea* ⟶	M	15
		Mark the statement that is *too broad* ⟶	B	5
		Mark the statement that is *too narrow* ⟶	N	5

a. Creative ideas can sometimes be very profitable. ☐ _____

b. Raising skunks as pets can be very profitable. ☐ _____

c. New ideas lead to success in business. ☐ _____

Score 15 points for each correct answer.   **Score**

Subject Matter

2 This passage is about

☐ a. the value of clever animals.

☐ b. profit from creativity.

☐ c. raising unusual pets.

☐ d. rare collections.   _____

Supporting Details

3 The insurance company wanted quills to

☐ a. make into unusual pens.

☐ b. be different from other companies.

☐ c. show new ideas to salesmen.

☐ d. use in its advertising campaign.   _____

Conclusion

4 This passage implies that

☐ a. people sometimes regret snap judgments.

☐ b. porcupines make poor pets.

☐ c. people will do anything for money.

☐ d. people with clever ideas can be successful.   _____

Clarifying Devices

5 The writer tells us about the porcupine quills because it

☐ a. adds interest to the passage.

☐ b. is a funny incident.

☐ c. is an example supporting his idea.

☐ d. is a story about animals.   _____

Vocabulary in Context

6 Grossed, as used in the passage, means

☐ a. huge.

☐ b. earned.

☐ c. found.

☐ d. invested.   _____

Add your scores for questions 1-6. Enter the total here and on the graph on page 238.

Total Score ☐

161

70

Alexander the Great

A horse named Bucephalus was offered for sale to Philip, King of Macedonia, in about 340 B.C. The king, his son, Alexander, and many others went to see it. The horse appeared extremely fierce. No one could mount it. King Philip was displeased and said, "Take this wild creature away." But Alexander said, "What a horse they are losing because they lack the skill and spirit to manage him!" Philip turned and said, "Young man, you find fault with your elders as if you know more than they, or could manage the horse better."

The prince quietly replied, "I know I can manage the horse better."

"If you should not be able to ride him, what will you forfeit?"

"I will pay the price of the horse."

The king agreed to the bet. Alexander grasped the horse's bridle and quickly turned him toward the sun so he would not see his shadow, which was what had disturbed him. While the spirited horse pranced, Alexander spoke softly and stroked him. Then he leaped lightly upon the horse's back. Without pulling the reins too hard or using a whip or spurs, he set Bucephalus to running. He pushed him on to a full gallop. Philip and his court looked on in great fear.

At the end of the field, Alexander suddenly wheeled the horse and raced back at tremendous speed. Loud shouts broke out from the group. Alexander's father, weeping with joy, kissed him and said, "My son, seek ye another kingdom that may be worthy of thy abilities, for Macedonia is too small for thee."

Main Idea 1

	Answer	Score
Mark the *main idea* ⟶	M	15
Mark the statement that is *too broad* ⟶	B	5
Mark the statement that is *too narrow* ⟶	N	5
a. Alexander knew how to tame horses.	☐	
b. King Philip learned that Alexander had qualities that would make him great.	☐	
c. People with strength and courage can tame wild horses.	☐	

Score 15 points for each correct answer.   **Score**

Subject Matter

2 This passage is about

☐ a. how Macedonians trained horses.

☐ b. a son being disrespectful to his father.

☐ c. a story that showed Alexander's great strength of character.

☐ d. a boy named Alexander and his horse Bucephalus.

_____

Supporting Details

3 Alexander was able to manage the horse because he

☐ a. was the king's son.

☐ b. was stern and harsh with the animal.

☐ c. was afraid of losing the bet with his father.

☐ d. noticed something about the horse that others missed.

_____

Conclusion 4 The horse's name, Bucephalus, is Greek for "ox-head." Based on the passage, you could infer that

☐ a. the Macedonians thought oxen more beautiful than horses.

☐ b. Bucephalus looked like an ox.

☐ c. perhaps the horse was "as stubborn as an ox."

☐ d. there was no particular reason for the name. _____

Clarifying Devices

5 The author develops the main idea of this passage through the use of

☐ a. detailed descriptions.

☐ b. narration of facts.

☐ c. comparisons.

☐ d. dramatic dialogue.

_____

Vocabulary in Context

6 The word <u>spirited</u> is used to mean

☐ a. ghostly.

☐ b. skittish.

☐ c. lively.

☐ d. religious.

_____

Add your scores for questions 1-6. Enter the total here and on the graph on page 238.   **Total Score** ☐

71

Plants Without Soil

In the Arizona desert, tomatoes hang from ceilings, spinach grows without soil and shrimp live in indoor pools. What's going on? Food research!

People perform these experiments to learn how to produce more food. By the year 2000 there will be over 6.5 billion people on earth. We will have to produce four times as much food as we do now to feed all these people. But each year there is less fresh water, the soil loses nutrients and buildings take up more land. We must learn to use resources we have always thought unusable. So, the Environmental Research Laboratory in Arizona tries to grow food without soil, in the desert, and with salt water.

So far the results have been excellent. The new methods yield twenty times more tomatoes and cucumbers than can be grown on a farm. About sixty times as many shrimp can be raised in indoor pools than ten boats can catch in the ocean in a year. Crops can grow in salty soil. Plus, as they grow, they take salt and minerals from desert soil, to create more usuable land.

The University of Arizona runs the research center in Arizona. But there are centers all over the world. Because of the promising results, big companies pay for some of the research. With interest and money backing them, researchers can go far. Their aim is to use wasted land and water to feed humanity. In the Arizona desert, they are off to a great start.

Main Idea	1		Answer	Score
		Mark the *main idea* ⟶	M	15
		Mark the statement that is *too broad* ⟶	B	5
		Mark the statement that is *too narrow* ⟶	N	5

a. The University of Arizona is doing food research in the Arizona desert. ☐ _____

b. Researchers study food and nutrition. ☐ _____

c. Scientists are trying to grow food on land and in water that is now wasted. ☐ _____

Score 15 points for each correct answer.   **Score**

Subject Matter

2 This passage focuses on

☐ a. new ways to grow spinach.
☐ b. the population explosion.
☐ c. research to produce more food.
☐ d. desert farming.

_____

Supporting Details

3 People must produce more food because

☐ a. people get hungrier every year.
☐ b. the population of the world is growing.
☐ c. there are too many unemployed farmers.
☐ d. people do not like the food now produced.

_____

Conclusion

4 It seems the author of this passage hopes

☐ a. population growth slows down.
☐ b. large companies donate more money to research.
☐ c. the supply of fresh water increases.
☐ d. scientists can find a way to solve the food problem.

_____

Clarifying Devices

5 The first paragraph catches the reader's attention with

☐ a. dramatic facts.
☐ b. a firsthand story.
☐ c. an emotional appeal.
☐ d. sharply contrasting ideas.

_____

Vocabulary in Context

6 In this passage yield means

☐ a. slow down.
☐ b. to give in to pressure.
☐ c. to produce.
☐ d. to compromise.

_____

Add your scores for questions 1-6. Enter the total here and on the graph on page 238.   **Total Score** ☐

72

Vipers

The family of snakes called vipers includes some of the deadliest poisonous snakes in the world. Some of the snakes in this fearsome group are the water moccasin, rattlesnake, and copperhead, all found in the United States, the bushmaster and fer-de-lance of South America, and the puff adder of Africa.

Vipers have thick bodies, short tails and triangular heads. Fangs in their upper jaws inject poison into their victims' bodies like a hypodermic needle. When the snakes bite, they contract the muscles around their poison sacs. These sacs are located behind the eyes. The poison squirts out through the hollow fangs. Almost a half-teaspoon of poison is put into a victim at one time. Fortunately, many of these snakes are small, so their bite is not fatal.

There are actually two main types of vipers—the true vipers and the pit vipers. Pit vipers live in Asia and the Americas. The name comes from a small hollow in the side of the head just below the eye. The small hollow, or pit, has a special nerve that senses heat, helping the pit viper to find its warm-blooded prey. True vipers don't have this special nerve and must rely on their <u>keen</u> sense of smell to find their food. Vipers don't usually strike unless they are disturbed or are looking for food. Still, it is a good idea to stay away from them.

Main Idea 1

	Answer	Score
Mark the *main idea* ⟶	M	15
Mark the statement that is *too broad* ⟶	B	5
Mark the statement that is *too narrow* ⟶	N	5
a. Many snakes are poisonous.	☐	_____
b. Vipers are one of the most poisonous groups of snakes.	☐	_____
c. Some vipers are called pit vipers.	☐	_____

Score 15 points for each correct answer.   Score

Subject Matter

2 This passage is about
- ☐ a. turning vipers into pets.
- ☐ b. how to cure snakebites.
- ☐ c. poisonous snakes of the world.
- ☐ d. vipers.

_____

Supporting Details

3 Which of the following is <u>not</u> true?
- ☐ a. The bushmaster is from South America.
- ☐ b. Some vipers have hollows like pits.
- ☐ c. Pit vipers are found in Africa.
- ☐ d. A viper's fangs are hollow.

_____

Conclusion

4 We can infer from the passage that
- ☐ a. all snakes with triangular heads are vipers.
- ☐ b. small vipers are harmless because of small amounts of venom.
- ☐ c. very long snakes are not vipers.
- ☐ d. when snakes are extremely hungry they eat people.

_____

Clarifying Devices

5 The author compares the viper's poison-injecting fangs to
- ☐ a. a squirt gun.
- ☐ b. a hypodermic needle.
- ☐ c. triangular needles.
- ☐ d. biting machines.

_____

Vocabulary in Context

6 The word <u>keen</u> means
- ☐ a. really nice.
- ☐ b. eager.
- ☐ c. vivid.
- ☐ d. very sensitive.

_____

Add your scores for questions 1-6. Enter the total here and on the graph on page 238.

Total Score ☐

Watch Out for Quicksand!

While hiking in the swamplands of Florida, Fred Stahl watched Jack Pickett disappear before his eyes. Pickett had stepped onto what looked like an <u>innocent</u> patch of dry sand and then started to sink. Within fifteen minutes, Pickett had disappeared completely beneath the surface.

Pickett was a victim of quicksand. If you think quicksand is something found only in adventure novels or films, you're making a big mistake. And that mistake could cost you your life.

Geologist Gerard H. Matthes, who once escaped from quicksand himself, always gave this message to hikers: "Anyone who ever walks off the pavement should learn about quicksand." It can be found almost anywhere.

Here are some of Matthes' tips on how to prevent being helplessly sucked under by quicksand. First of all, if you step into quicksand that is firm enough, you may be able to run out. But you have to move fast. If, however, the sand pulls your legs in too quickly for you to escape this way, throw yourself flat on your back. That's right—you can actually float in quicksand. Don't make the common mistake of raising your arms. Resting on the surface, your arms can help you to float. Any movements you make should be slow and deliberate. Quick, jerky movements can cause you to be completely sucked in, just as Jack Pickett was. Try doing a slow breaststroke or slowly rolling yourself to firm ground. Above all, don't panic.

Main Idea 1

Mark the *main idea* → M — 15

Mark the statement that is *too broad* → B — 5

Mark the statement that is *too narrow* → N — 5

a. Quicksand exists in many places, and you should know how to deal with it. ☐ ____

b. A hiker named Pickett was sucked into quicksand in the Florida swamps. ☐ ____

c. There are many natural dangers that you should know about. ☐ ____

Score 15 points for each correct answer.   **Score**

Subject Matter **2** This passage is mainly about

☐ a. where quicksand is found.

☐ b. what causes quicksand.

☐ c. the facts about quicksand.

☐ d. dangers in the wilderness.   _____

Supporting Details **3** When stepping into quicksand, you should first try to run out because

☐ a. most quicksand is slower in trapping a victim than commonly believed.

☐ b. the sand may be firm enough to allow escape this way.

☐ c. it can't trap you if you keep moving.

☐ d. this is the only way you can escape.   _____

Conclusion **4** The passage implies that quicksand

☐ a. is found mostly in swamp areas.

☐ b. permits no escape.

☐ c. is only found in books and movies.

☐ d. is a serious danger.   _____

Clarifying Devices **5** In the first paragraph, the writer creates interest by using a

☐ a. dramatic example.

☐ b. broad statement.

☐ c. surprising comparison.

☐ d. humorous story.   _____

Vocabulary in Context **6** As used in the first paragraph, <u>innocent</u> means

☐ a. almost bare.

☐ b. very pure.

☐ c. not dangerous.

☐ d. highly dangerous.   _____

Add your scores for questions 1-6. Enter the total here and on the graph on page 238.

Total Score ☐

74

Underwater Helper

It is a predator armed with 200 sharp teeth that could snap off a person's arm in just one bite. It eats eighteen to twenty pounds of fish and squid per day. An expert swimmer, it knifes through the water at twenty miles per hour. It can grow up to fourteen feet long and weigh up to 1,000 pounds. No, it isn't the fearsome shark. It's a sea mammal that may someday rival the dog as man's best friend: the dolphin.

Although they have the equipment to be killers, attacks by dolphins on human beings are unheard of. In fact, dolphins are being trained to work with people in a type of underwater teamwork. At the Makapuu Oceanic Center in Hawaii, dolphins are being trained as <u>couriers</u>, carrying tools and messages between men on boats and divers down below.

Dolphins are uniquely qualified for this task because of their sonar, or echo-location system. Dolphins fire sound impulses from air sacs in their heads. These impulses rebound off solid objects, allowing the animals to accurately detect moving objects from great distances, without having to see them. Within a range of fifty feet, a dolphin can determine the size, body makeup, and perhaps even the speed, of any object.

Scientists believe dolphins can be trained to work with people because of their intelligence. The size of a dolphin's brain in relation to its body weight is very high. Most experts place the dolphin's IQ between that of a dog and a chimpanzee.

Main Idea	1		Answer	Score
		Mark the *main idea* ⟶	M	15
		Mark the statement that is *too broad* ⟶	B	5.
		Mark the statement that is *too narrow* ⟶	N	5

a. Dolphins are being trained to work with people. ☐ _____

b. Mammals have large brains. ☐ _____

c. Dolphins are well-suited to work with people. ☐ _____

Score 15 points for each correct answer.
Score

Subject Matter

2 Another good title for this passage would be

- ☐ a. Science and the Sea.
- ☐ b. How Dolphins Use Sonar.
- ☐ c. The Dolphin—A New Best Friend for People.
- ☐ d. The Fearsome Dolphin. _____

Supporting Details

3 A dolphin's sonar allows it to

- ☐ a. protect itself from sharks.
- ☐ b. find tools dropped by divers.
- ☐ c. send messages.
- ☐ d. detect objects. _____

Conclusion

4 The passage suggests that dolphins

- ☐ a. have the potential to be very helpful to people.
- ☐ b. can be as dangerous as sharks.
- ☐ c. may replace dogs as pets.
- ☐ d. can be trained to use tools. _____

Clarifying Devices

5 In the first paragraph, the writer draws the reader in by

- ☐ a. keeping the identity of the subject a secret.
- ☐ b. presenting little-known facts about a fish.
- ☐ c. setting up a rivalry between dogs and dolphins.
- ☐ d. scaring the reader into thinking about sharks. _____

Vocabulary in Context

6 The best substitution for the word <u>couriers</u> would be

- ☐ a. cables.
- ☐ b. divers.
- ☐ c. messengers.
- ☐ d. lifelines. _____

Add your scores for questions 1-6. Enter the total here and on the graph on page 238.

Total Score ☐

75

Cover Your Eyes!

Nature has devised many ways to protect creatures' eyes. The most common protection is the eyelid—a fold of skin that closes over the eye, protecting it from damage. Eyelashes are useful for keeping out dust and other irritants, and tears wash away any particles that get through the other defenses.

Some creatures, including most birds, have three eyelids. The upper and lower lids act like human lids and keep out twigs, dirt and sand. The third eyelid, however, is a semitransparent tissue that crosses over the eye from the inside corner to the outside corner. Because of this protective membrane, birds seldom have to blink. They close their eyes only when they go to sleep. In ducks, this third eyelid serves as an underwater diving mask that helps the ducks find food.

Most fish and snakes have no eyelids at all. Instead, a hard glassy covering protects their eyes. In fish, water constantly sweeps away dirt from the covering. And a snake's eyesight is usually so bad that a little dirt obscuring its vision does not disturb it greatly.

Eyelashes defend the eye by shading it from glare. They also act like miniature brushes to remove dust. Camels have lashes that are four inches long to protect their eyes from windblown sand in the desert.

Main Idea   1

	Answer	Score
Mark the *main idea* ⟶	M	15
Mark the statement that is *too broad* ⟶	B	5
Mark the statement that is *too narrow* ⟶	N	5

a. Creatures' eyes are protected in a number of different ways. ☐ _____

b. Nature has provided many kinds of protection for living creatures. ☐ _____

c. Eyelids are one of the most important forms of eye protection. ☐ _____

Subject Matter **2** Another good title for this passage would be
- ☐ a. Look Out!
- ☐ b. Birds' Eyes.
- ☐ c. Eyes in the Night.
- ☐ d. Protecting the Eye.   _____

Supporting Details **3** A camel has long eyelashes
- ☐ a. to keep windblown sand out of its eyes.
- ☐ b. that get in the way of its sight.
- ☐ c. to help it see better.
- ☐ d. to attract other camels.   _____

Conclusion **4** The writer implies that eyelids are
- ☐ a. not found on lizards.
- ☐ b. nice to look at.
- ☐ c. always covered with eyelashes.
- ☐ d. the most effective eye protection.   _____

Clarifying Devices **5** The author compares the duck's third eyelid to a
- ☐ a. tissue.
- ☐ b. glass covering.
- ☐ c. tiny brush.
- ☐ d. diving mask.   _____

Vocabulary in Context **6** Obscuring in this selection means
- ☐ a. hiding.
- ☐ b. blocking.
- ☐ c. confusing.
- ☐ d. delaying.   _____

Add your scores for questions 1-6. Enter the total here and on the graph on page 238.   **Total Score** ☐

173

76

The Badger

The badger is a member of the weasel family. It ranges throughout the western United States. It is both a help and a burden to farmers and ranchers. It kills harmful rodents, but it also digs deep holes that cause tractors to break wheels and livestock to break legs.

A clumsy critter, the slow-footed badger is built low to the ground, with short legs and a flat, squat body. It digs like a steam shovel into the rich earth of the Dakota prairie. Its strong dark feet, each tipped with five two-inch-long nails, can dig any gopher or ground squirrel out of its burrow.

This pigeon-toed, round-shouldered ground hugger is dirty yellowish gray with a dark brown face striped with white. It may grow to more than two feet long and weigh up to twenty-five pounds. The badger has thirty-four sharp teeth and a menacing growl and hiss that make it about as sociable as a grizzly bear. Being a close cousin to the skunk, it doesn't smell very good.

An acute sense of smell enables the badger to locate food underground. It eats snakes and snails, insects, rats and mice, gophers, ground squirrels and other rodents. Occasionally it will kill ground-nesting birds and eat their nestlings or eggs, but the badger saves many more birds than it destroys. The rodents it usually kills are animals that hunt birds. And the holes it digs in its <u>quest</u> for food provide homes for many animals.

Main Idea   1

	Answer	Score
Mark the *main idea* ⟶	M	15
Mark the statement that is *too broad* ⟶	B	5
Mark the statement that is *too narrow* ⟶	N	5

a. The badger lives in the western United States and is considered both a help and a burden. ☐ _____

b. Prairie animals can be both helpful and harmful. ☐ _____

c. The badger hunts many rodents that live on the prairie. ☐ _____

Score 15 points for each correct answer. **Score**

Subject Matter **2** This passage is about

    ☐ a. the problems of farmers.

    ☐ b. the badger.

    ☐ c. rodents.

    ☐ d. prairie animals. _____

Supporting Details **3** According to the passage, the badger's smell

    ☐ a. is bad and helps to make it unsociable.

    ☐ b. is stronger than a skunk's smell.

    ☐ c. attracts rodents and snakes.

    ☐ d. is feared more than its sharp teeth. _____

Conclusion **4** The passage suggests that badgers

    ☐ a. are pleasant animals.

    ☐ b. are a nuisance to foxes and coyotes.

    ☐ c. aren't friendly animals.

    ☐ d. are lazy. _____

Clarifying Devices **5** The writer of this passage tells this story by depending mainly on

    ☐ a. cases cited by farmers and ranchers.

    ☐ b. logical reasoning and careful argument.

    ☐ c. carefully chosen adjectives and adverbs.

    ☐ d. facts given by scientists. _____

Vocabulary in Context **6** Quest means

    ☐ a. need.

    ☐ b. adventure.

    ☐ c. battle.

    ☐ d. search. _____

Add your scores for questions 1-6. Enter the total here and on the graph on page 238.

Total Score ☐

175

77

Once Poison, Now a Food

Would you eat a bacon, lettuce and love apple sandwich? You probably have eaten many of them. Love apple was the name used many years ago for the tomato.

The tomato is originally an American plant. It was found in South America by early Spanish explorers. The word *tomato* comes from the native Nahuatl word *tomatl*. But when it moved north, the plant earned a different name. Remarkably, the settlers in North America thought it was poisonous. They believed that to eat it was surely to die. It was said that jilted <u>suitors</u> would threaten to eat a tomato to cause their cold-hearted lovers remorse. Because of this legend, the settlers called the tomato a "love apple." While people enjoyed other native plants such as corn and sweet potatoes, everyone avoided the tomato.

No one knows who first dared to eat a tomato. Perhaps someone was brave enough, or lovesick enough, to try out the truth of the rumors. Of course, whoever ate this fruit was perfectly safe. No one died from eating a love apple. Still, it was many years before the people fully believed that the tomato was a safe, and even good, food. But its use did become common, and the plant was sent across the ocean to become part of many traditional European dishes.

		Answer	Score
Main Idea	**1**		
	Mark the *main idea* ⟶	**M**	15
	Mark the statement that is *too broad* ⟶	**B**	5
	Mark the statement that is *too narrow* ⟶	**N**	5

a. Many foods have legends associated with them. ☐ _____

b. Although the tomato was thought to be poisonous, no one died from eating it. ☐ _____

c. Long ago the tomato was called a "love apple" and was thought to be poisonous. ☐ _____

Subject Matter **2** Another good title for this passage would be
- [ ] a. Life in Early America.
- [ ] b. What Happens to the Brokenhearted.
- [ ] c. The History of the Tomato.
- [ ] d. Vegetables in Our Diet. _____

Supporting Details **3** The language from which we derived the word *tomato* is
- [ ] a. Portuguese.
- [ ] b. Spanish.
- [ ] c. Nahuatl.
- [ ] d. European. _____

Conclusion **4** North American people didn't eat tomatoes at first because
- [ ] a. they had too much other food.
- [ ] b. they mistakenly thought they were poisonous.
- [ ] c. settlers ate only traditional European foods.
- [ ] d. no one liked the taste. _____

Clarifying Devices **5** The word *still* in the middle of the third paragraph tells you that
- [ ] a. people continue to be wary of tomatoes.
- [ ] b. people became very quiet when speaking of tomatoes.
- [ ] c. the sentence contains information that will modify the idea of the previous sentence.
- [ ] d. the sentence is going to tell you something entirely different about tomatoes. _____

Vocabulary in Context **6** Suitor means
- [ ] a. boyfriend.
- [ ] b. launderer.
- [ ] c. tailor.
- [ ] d. explorer. _____

Add your scores for questions 1-6. Enter the total here and on the graph on page 238. **Total Score** [ ]

78

The Man from Stratford

What makes a person famous? This is a mystery that many people have pondered. All kinds of myths surround the lives of well-known people.

Most people are familiar with the works of William Shakespeare, one of the greatest English writers of the sixteenth century. Yet how many know Shakespeare the person, the man behind the works?

After centuries of research, scholars are still trying to discover Shakespeare's personal history. It is not easily found in his writings. Authors of the time could not protect their works. An acting company, for example, could change a play if they wanted to. Nowadays writers have copyrights that protect their work.

Many myths arose about Shakespeare. Some said he had no <u>formal</u> education. There are rumors that he left home when accused of stealing a horse. Others believe that he began his career by tending the horses of wealthy men.

All of these myths are interesting, but are they true? Probably not. Shakespeare's father was a respected man in Stratford, a member of the town council. He sent young William to grammar school. Most people of Elizabethan times did not continue beyond grammar school; so, Shakespeare did have, at least, an average education.

Some parts of Shakespeare's life will always remain unknown. The Great London Fire of 1666 burned many important documents that could have been a source of clues. We will always be left with many questions and few facts.

Main Idea	1		Answer	Score
	Mark the *main idea* ———————→		M	15
	Mark the statement that is *too broad* ——→		B	5
	Mark the statement that is *too narrow* ——→		N	5
	a. Very little is known about Shakespeare as a person.		☐	___
	b. Shakespeare's writings are all we have as clues about him.		☐	___
	c. Shakespeare's personal history will never be known.		☐	___

Score 15 points for each correct answer. **Score**

Subject Matter

2 This passage deals with

☐ a. the Great London Fire.

☐ b. the lost documents of Shakespeare.

☐ c. scholars of Shakespeare.

☐ d. Shakespeare's personal history. _____

Supporting Details

3 Parts of Shakespeare's life continue to remain a mystery because

☐ a. people are not interested.

☐ b. researchers do not have the expertise to find the facts.

☐ c. writers had no claim over their works.

☐ d. the Great London Fire burned important documents. _____

Conclusion

4 From this passage we can infer that Shakespeare

☐ a. was a horse thief.

☐ b. had no education.

☐ c. is surrounded by myths.

☐ d. was popular in Stratford. _____

Clarifying Devices

5 The first sentence arouses interest by presenting

☐ a. a direct statement.

☐ b. a question.

☐ c. an emotional appeal.

☐ d. a contrast. _____

Vocabulary in Context

6 In this passage formal means

☐ a. correct.

☐ b. organized.

☐ c. rigid.

☐ d. elaborate. _____

Add your scores for questions 1-6. Enter the total here and on the graph on page 238.

Total Score ☐

79

Jaws

Of all the fish in the ocean, sharks are the greediest eaters and killers. They suffer from <u>continual</u> hunger. Almost as soon as they have eaten, they are on the prowl for more food. Sharks have been described as eating machines, and indeed they are perfectly designed for that activity. They are powerful swimmers, with smooth, well-muscled, stream-lined bodies.

But the most remarkable part of a shark is its mouth—a wide gash lined with rows of jagged teeth. When a shark attacks, it opens its mouth wide until its teeth can stab straight into the body of its victim. The teeth slice like razors as the shark twists and rolls its body to tear off a chunk of food. New teeth are constantly being formed and moving forward to take the place of those lost during the shark's violent feeding activities. Even very old sharks have razor-sharp teeth.

The largest and most fearsome of the species is the great white shark. Its average length is between fourteen and sixteen feet. A few great whites may reach well over thirty feet in length. The longest ever recorded was a thirty-seven-footer, a truly monstrous fish. The great white lives in the tropical seas and sometimes along the southern coast of the United States.

Main Idea 1

	Answer	Score
Mark the *main idea* →	M	15
Mark the statement that is *too broad* →	B	5
Mark the statement that is *too narrow* →	N	5

a. Sharks are large ocean fish. ☐ _____

b. Sharks are greedy eaters. ☐ _____

c. Sharks are powerful fish that are well designed to hunt other fish for their food. ☐ _____

Score 15 points for each correct answer.   Score

Subject Matter

2 This passage is mostly about

☐ a. great white sharks.

☐ b. how sharks are designed for their eating needs.

☐ c. the way in which sharks grow new teeth.

☐ d. why so many people hate and fear sharks. _____

Supporting Details

3 Sharks tear off food by

☐ a. squeezing it.

☐ b. slicing it.

☐ c. killing it.

☐ d. rolling their bodies. _____

Conclusion

4 We can infer from this passage that

☐ a. even old sharks have no trouble eating.

☐ b. old sharks starve to death because of weak teeth.

☐ c. sharks fear people and will not go near them.

☐ d. sharks die young because they wear themselves out. _____

Clarifying Devices

5 "Jagged" teeth are

☐ a. dull.

☐ b. broken.

☐ c. sharp and uneven.

☐ d. large. _____

Vocabulary in Context

6 <u>Continual</u> means

☐ a. painful.

☐ b. fierce.

☐ c. constant.

☐ d. enormous. _____

Add your scores for questions 1-6. Enter the total here and on the graph on page 238.   Total Score ☐

80

Leaf-Cutters

A clean dirt path several inches wide is a sign that you are near a leaf-cutter ant colony. In one direction the path branches into trails that end at a tree trunk or peter out in the grass. In the other direction it leads to the colony's nest—a wide area marked by holes and large rubbish heaps.

The holes are entrances to the underground nest. The rubbish heaps are piles of old, dry plant matter that was cleared out of the nest when it was no longer useful. Leaf-cutters are farmers, and they use leaves and grass to grow their food—fungi. Fungi are plants that grow on other plants or on decaying matter. Toadstools and molds are types of fungi. At night the ants go out to <u>forage</u> for more material to grow food. Each ant carries a piece of leaf at least twice as large as its own body.

Leaf-cutters come in all sizes, and, oddly enough, it is the largest ones who do the least work. They are soldiers, whose main job is to protect the nest. They have enormous jaws. Because of this, the native Indians of South America, where these ants are found, put them to an odd use. Instead of using stitches to close a wound, the Indians hold large leaf-cutter ants up to the edges of a cut and let them bite it together. Then they pinch off the bodies, leaving the jaws behind to hold the wound firmly closed.

Main Idea   1

	Answer	Score
Mark the *main idea* ⟶	M	15
Mark the statement that is *too broad* ⟶	B	5
Mark the statement that is *too narrow* ⟶	N	5

a. The leaf-cutters are farmers that grow their food in dead plant material. ☐ _____

b. Leaf-cutter ants work hard to survive. ☐ _____

c. Leaf-cutters carry grass and leaves to their nests. ☐ _____

Score 15 points for each correct answer.   **Score**

Subject Matter

2 This passage is about
- ☐ a. fungi.
- ☐ b. leaf-cutter ants.
- ☐ c. South American Indians.
- ☐ d. farming.   _____

Supporting Details

3 Leaf-cutter ants eat
- ☐ a. bark from tree trunks.
- ☐ b. fungi.
- ☐ c. leaves and grass.
- ☐ d. decaying matter.   _____

Conclusion

4 This passage implies that
- ☐ a. leaf-cutter ants work harder than other ants.
- ☐ b. leaf-cutter ants are small.
- ☐ c. the largest ants do not help grow food for the colony.
- ☐ d. anyone can find a leaf-cutter ant colony.   _____

Clarifying Devices

5 The phrase "oddly enough" indicates
- ☐ a. from a human point of view it's strange that the strongest ants do the least work.
- ☐ b. small ants are lazy when compared with the larger ones.
- ☐ c. that the ants vary in size tremendously, depending on their jobs.
- ☐ d. that it's odd that leaf-cutters come in all sizes.   _____

Vocabulary in Context

6 To <u>forage</u> means to
- ☐ a. plant.
- ☐ b. work.
- ☐ c. search.
- ☐ d. beg.   _____

Add your scores for questions 1-6. Enter the total here and on the graph on page 238.   **Total Score** [ ]

81

A Deal Is a Deal!

When Abraham Lincoln was a lawyer in rural Illinois, he and a certain judge in town once got to <u>bantering</u> with one another about horse trading. The upshot of the discussion was that they agreed that the next morning, at nine o'clock, they would meet in front of the general store and make a trade. Each would bring a horse, unseen by anyone up to that hour. If either backed out of the deal, he would forfeit $25. The money from each man was held by the local banker.

The next morning, at the appointed hour, the Judge came up the dirt road, leading the sorriest looking specimen of a horse ever seen in those parts of Illinois. The large crowd viewing the spectacle burst out laughing, already knowing that Abe Lincoln was bound to get the worst of the deal. A poorer horse just couldn't exist anywhere and still be walking.

In a few minutes, however, Mr. Lincoln was seen approaching the general store carrying something quite large and bulky on his shoulders. As he drew nearer, the crowd saw what it was, and great shouts and laughter broke out. The shouts and laughter soon broke into a thunderous roar when Mr. Lincoln, looking carefully and seriously over the Judge's animal, set down his sawhorse, and exclaimed, "Well, Judge, this is the first time I ever got the worst of it in a horse trade."

Main Idea   **1**

	Answer	Score
Mark the *main idea* ⟶	**M**	15
Mark the statement that is *too broad* ⟶	**B**	5
Mark the statement that is *too narrow* ⟶	**N**	5

a. Abe Lincoln possessed a terrific sense of humor. ☐ _____

b. Mr. Lincoln was a popular man. ☐ _____

c. The Judge must have had a sense of humor. ☐ _____

Score 15 points for each correct answer.   Score

Subject Matter

2 This passage concerns
- ☐ a. the life of Abe Lincoln.
- ☐ b. a horse trade made by Abe Lincoln.
- ☐ c. gambling.
- ☐ d. Abe Lincoln's philosophy.   _____

Supporting Details

3 The horse Abe Lincoln brought was
- ☐ a. sick.
- ☐ b. wild.
- ☐ c. wooden.
- ☐ d. small.   _____

Conclusion

4 It is evident that neither Lincoln nor the Judge was
- ☐ a. serious about their agreement.
- ☐ b. a native of Illinois.
- ☐ c. very knowledgeable about horses.
- ☐ d. in the mood for jokes.   _____

Clarifying Devices

5 This passage attempts to provoke
- ☐ a. outrage.
- ☐ b. tears.
- ☐ c. sympathy.
- ☐ d. laughter.   _____

Vocabulary in Context

6 A person who banters is
- ☐ a. singing.
- ☐ b. insulting.
- ☐ c. talking.
- ☐ d. deceiving.   _____

Add your scores for questions 1-6. Enter the total here and on the graph on page 239.   Total Score ☐

82

The Witch's Wind

In California it's called the "Santa Ana." Argentinians call it the "zonda." It has more than twenty other local names; one of the most fitting is the "witch's wind." The scientific name for this mysterious wind is *foehn*, pronounced *fern*.

A foehn is a moving mass of air which, after crossing mountains, becomes a dry, gusty wind that moves with great power. A witch's wind in Texas once flattened 252 oil derricks. One in Austria derailed three streetcars, each weighing over three tons.

There is an unresolved mystery in the witch's wind. The foehn can have a strange and hard-to-explain effect on people's physical and mental states. When the wind is blowing, some people experience what in Europe is called "the foehn disease." Those who suffer from it say they are depressed and can't concentrate. In Germany, you can even buy anti-foehn pills.

In many places, there have been increases in the numbers of accidents, suicides and calls for medical help during the wind. The foehn has been blamed for everything from drops in factory production to family quarrels. In California during the 1890s, people who committed crimes of passion during the witch's wind could use the foehn as an excuse.

Some people feel symptoms even before the wind arrives. They may have headaches or breathing problems. Their skin becomes taut, and old scars ache. These signs have occurred in people as much as ten hours before scientific weather equipment detected the foehn's approach.

Main Idea	1		Answer	Score
	Mark the *main idea* ⟶		M	15
	Mark the statement that is *too broad* ⟶		B	5
	Mark the statement that is *too narrow* ⟶		N	5
	a. The witch's wind has a strong and mysterious effect on people.		☐	___
	b. The witch's wind has great destructive force.		☐	___
	c. Weather changes can produce mysterious mental effects.		☐	___

Score 15 points for each correct answer. Score

Subject Matter

2 The passage is mainly about
- ☐ a. the destructive power of wind.
- ☐ b. different types of winds.
- ☐ c. how weather affects people.
- ☐ d. foehns. _____

Supporting Details

3 The foehn is mysterious because
- ☐ a. of its power to lift great weights.
- ☐ b. its origin is unknown.
- ☐ c. it can affect physical and mental health.
- ☐ d. it occurs in many different areas of the world. _____

Conclusion

4 The passage implies that "witch's wind" is a good name for the foehn because
- ☐ a. the word *foehn* means "witch."
- ☐ b. it has a strange and harmful power.
- ☐ c. it causes depression.
- ☐ d. it has become legendary. _____

Clarifying Devices

5 The writer tells how the foehn "flattened 252 oil derricks" in order to
- ☐ a. impress the reader with the wind's power.
- ☐ b. explain the mystery of the foehn.
- ☐ c. emphasize how unpredictable the wind is.
- ☐ d. compare the foehn with other destructive natural forces. _____

Vocabulary in Context

6 As used in the passage, the word <u>states</u> means
- ☐ a. positions.
- ☐ b. declares.
- ☐ c. nations.
- ☐ d. conditions. _____

Add your scores for questions 1–6. Enter the total here and on the graph on page 239.

Total Score ☐

83

The Greatest Jumper

The world's best jumpers all come from Australia. Most Olympic athletes train for years before they succeed in making a twenty-foot long jump. But the kangaroo, the greatest jumper on earth, can travel in twenty-foot leaps, moving almost as fast as a car on the highway!

The kangaroo's build enables it to travel at this speed for long, long distances without stopping. Its small head and short front feet <u>reduce</u> resistance to the wind, giving the animal a streamlined appearance. All of the kangaroo's weight is concentrated on the back of its body—in the thick, long tail and the long hindquarters. The animal can sit on its tail as if it were a chair, or use it to maintain balance during long bounds. The kangaroo's hind feet, which are like springboards when it jumps, can be as long as ten inches from heel to toe.

Another interesting aspect of the kangaroo is its talent for boxing. When its front paws are dressed in boxing gloves, the kangaroo can deliver strong punches or hop around and completely tire the person out. But despite advantages in speed and endurance, the kangaroo will not hurt other animals and will eat only vegetables. And although the kangaroo can leap over five-foot fences as if they were nothing, it can't walk!

Main Idea   1

	Answer	Score
Mark the *main idea* ⟶	M	15
Mark the statement that is *too broad* ⟶	B	5
Mark the statement that is *too narrow* ⟶	N	5
a. Some animals can travel very fast.	☐	___
b. The kangaroo is the world's greatest jumper.	☐	___
c. The kangaroo is a good boxer.	☐	___

Score 15 points for each correct answer. Score

Subject Matter **2** This passage is concerned with

☐ a. runners and boxers.

☐ b. the kangaroo.

☐ c. Australia.

☐ d. jumping over fences. _____

Supporting Details **3** Although the kangaroo can beat a person in boxing, it can't

☐ a. walk.

☐ b. race as fast as a car.

☐ c. jump long distances.

☐ d. jump over fences. _____

Conclusion **4** The kangaroo can jump so rapidly because its

☐ a. survival depends on speed.

☐ b. body is ideally built for it.

☐ c. parents trained it.

☐ d. constant practice developed strong muscles. _____

Clarifying Devices **5** The author develops the main idea by

☐ a. using examples.

☐ b. telling separate kangaroo stories.

☐ c. citing research data.

☐ d. describing the animal. _____

Vocabulary in Context **6** Reduce, in this passage, means

☐ a. cut down on.

☐ b. lose weight.

☐ c. shrink.

☐ d. increase. _____

Add your scores for questions 1-6. Enter the total here and on the graph on page 239. Total Score ☐

189

84

The Great Hunter

An owl uses its talons and beak to catch and kill its prey, but these are not its most important weapons in the hunt. What makes the owl such a deadly hunter are its eyes and ears.

An owl's eyes can pick up the faintest glimmer of light or the least little movement from its prey. The pupils can be opened or closed independently of each other, allowing an owl to see equally well in the bright sun with one eye and in dark shadows with the other at the same time. This serves as an important aid for those species that hunt during the day in a forest spotted with sun and shade.

Even with no light at all, an owl can detect a mouse and swoop down on it accurately, using only its keen sense of hearing. Thus, it can <u>home</u> in on the sound of a mouse chewing seeds, even if the mouse is hidden under a layer of leaves or snow.

The owl can also remain motionless on its perch while twisting its head as much as three-quarters of the way around its body, searching for the source of a faint sound or a flicker of movement from its intended prey.

Main Idea	1		Answer	Score
	Mark the *main idea* ⟶		M	15
	Mark the statement that is *too broad* ⟶		B	5
	Mark the statement that is *too narrow* ⟶		N	5

a. Owls rely on their keen sight and hearing to find their prey. ☐ _____

b. Owls are very effective hunters. ☐ _____

c. Owls can detect prey by using their hearing alone. ☐ _____

Score 15 points for each correct answer.   **Score**

Subject Matter

2 This passage focuses on the owl's
- ☐ a. flexibility.
- ☐ b. hunting weapons.
- ☐ c. talons.
- ☐ d. prey.   _____

Supporting Details

3 Which of the following is <u>not</u> true? The owl's eyes
- ☐ a. see equally well in sun or shade.
- ☐ b. are independent of each other.
- ☐ c. can pick up the slightest movement of its prey.
- ☐ d. are keener than its ears.   _____

Conclusion

4 We can conclude from the passage that owls are
- ☐ a. wise parents.
- ☐ b. sharp hunters.
- ☐ c. cute when young.
- ☐ d. lazy when old.   _____

Clarifying Devices

5 The function of the first sentence in this passage is to
- ☐ a. throw the reader off the right track.
- ☐ b. bring out the negative arguments.
- ☐ c. de-emphasize the talons and beak of an owl as weapons.
- ☐ d. bring out the logical reasoning.   _____

Vocabulary in Context

6 <u>Home</u> in this passage means
- ☐ a. channel.
- ☐ b. burrow.
- ☐ c. dig.
- ☐ d. detect the position.   _____

Add your scores for questions 1-6. Enter the total here and on the graph on page 239.   **Total Score** ☐

85

Garlic: The Magic Cure-All

Once you have smelled the delicious aroma of garlic, you'll never forget it. It is an herb that is widely used in cooking and salads. You may hear of people using it to improve their health. Some say it even has magical powers. These magical powers were known of even in ancient times. For instance, a Roman soldier would not go into battle without first eating some garlic. The Romans believed that garlic gave a person strength and courage. Whether or not the soldiers fought any better because of their garlic eating, however, is unknown. Nevertheless, this Roman habit may have been frightening to the enemies.

The period of the Middle Ages was <u>fraught</u> with superstition. During the frightening Black Plague, people ate bushels of garlic as protection against the dread disease. Garlic was thought of as a cure-all. For example, people who feared vampires, werewolves and the evil eye of a witch would wear cloves of garlic wrapped in cloth and hung around their necks.

Even today, garlic is used in various old-fashioned, cure-all remedies. A syrup made from garlic is said to cure colds. A clove of garlic wrapped in a wet cloth and kept on the chest will relieve the discomforts of bronchitis. Garlic has even been put to use in agriculture. Garlic scattered in the soil around peach trees is supposed to protect the trees from harmful borers. And garlic really can be soothing when rubbed on insect bites.

In actuality, garlic's value is not all superstition. Garlic does contain an antibiotic, allium, which doctors use to lower high blood pressure in patients.

Main Idea	1		Answer	Score
		Mark the *main idea* →	M	15
		Mark the statement that is *too broad* →	B	5
		Mark the statement that is *too narrow* →	N	5
		a. Many superstitions surround the use of garlic.	☐	____
		b. Garlic was a main ingredient in many old-fashioned remedies.	☐	____
		c. Some people believe that certain herbs have magical powers.	☐	____

Score 15 points for each correct answer.   **Score**

Subject Matter

2 This passage discusses the uses of

☐ a. allium.
☐ b. superstition.
☐ c. garlic.
☐ d. magic herbs.   _____

Supporting Details

3 The allium contained in garlic is good for

☐ a. diabetes.
☐ b. high blood pressure.
☐ c. headaches.
☐ d. ulcers.   _____

Conclusion

4 It is evident from this passage that

☐ a. garlic has magical powers.
☐ b. the Roman soldiers owed their victories to garlic.
☐ c. garlic has had many uses throughout history.
☐ d. garlic is a valuable cure-all medicine.   _____

Clarifying Devices

5 The writer shows the diverse uses of garlic by

☐ a. giving examples.
☐ b. tracing its evolution.
☐ c. speculating.
☐ d. proving its value.   _____

Vocabulary in Context

6 As used in this passage, the word <u>fraught</u> means

☐ a. devoid.
☐ b. characterized.
☐ c. scattered.
☐ d. full of.   _____

Add your scores for questions 1-6. Enter the total here and on the graph on page 239.

Total Score ☐

86

I Wouldn't Try It Again

He shouldn't have come back alive. Captain J.H. Hedley was a British pilot in World War I. He fell victim to a bit of misfortune that would have been enough to kill anyone. Yet, with bad luck staring him in the face, good luck was coming up fast on his tail.

Captain Hedley was flying a mission over Germany with his copilot, a Canadian flyer named Makepeace. Suddenly they were surrounded by a group of German fighters. Makepeace, an experienced pilot, knew he had to take the plane into a vertical dive in order to slip away from the Germans. Inexplicably, Hedley was caught unaware by his copilot's maneuver. He was thrown sharply out of his seat and out of the plane. Makepeace sadly counted Hedley a dead man and continued his evasive maneuvers.

Suddenly, Makepeace spotted Hedley clinging to the tail of the plane. Hedley hung on and pulled himself back into the plane when it leveled off. Makepeace was stunned by the sight of Hedley, but he kept his composure enough to get them out of trouble and out of Germany. The best explanation for Hedley's reprieve was that the plane's sudden vertical dive had created a vacuum in the air behind it. Hedley fell into the vacuum and was pulled along until he grabbed the tail and made his fantastic reentry.

Main Idea 1

	Answer	Score
Mark the *main idea* ———→	M	15
Mark the statement that is *too broad* ——→	B	5
Mark the statement that is *too narrow* ——→	N	5

a. Captain Hedley was thrown from an open cockpit plane. ☐ ____

b. People sometimes miraculously survive terribly dangerous accidents. ☐ ____

c. Captain Hedley was thrown out of an airplane and was able to get back inside unharmed. ☐ ____

Score 15 points for each correct answer.   Score

Subject Matter

2 This passage is about

☐ a. World War II.

☐ b. the adventures of Makepeace and Hedley.

☐ c. the miraculous fall and recovery of Captain Hedley.

☐ d. World War I.   _____

Supporting Details

3 In World War I, Britain and Canada were

☐ a. afraid of each other.

☐ b. in competition.

☐ c. allies.

☐ d. fighting each other.   _____

Conclusion

4 We can conclude that Hedley's escape from death was mostly due to

☐ a. faith.

☐ b. luck.

☐ c. science.

☐ d. Makepeace's flying ability.   _____

Clarifying Devices

5 The writer begins the passage by

☐ a. making a series of interesting statements without explaining them.

☐ b. telling a joke.

☐ c. asking some questions.

☐ d. quoting a war veteran.   _____

Vocabulary in Context

6 Something <u>inexplicable</u> is

☐ a. ridiculous.

☐ b. memorable.

☐ c. unforgivable.

☐ d. unexplainable.   _____

Add your scores for questions 1-6. Enter the total here and on the graph on page 239.

Total Score ☐

195

87

Fire Is Fearsome

People often speak of fire as though it were a living creature—it grows, dances, needs oxygen, feeds on whatever it can find, and then dies. And when a forest fire rages out of control, threatening human lives and homes, it must be fought like a "wild animal." The fight is often desperate, since firefighters' best efforts may be dwarfed by the fury of a large fire. But the fire's own traits can be used against it.

The heated air above a fire rises in a pillar of smoke and burnt gases, pulling fresh air in from the sides to replace it. Firefighters use this fact when they "fight fire with fire." They start a fire well in front of the one which they are fighting. Instead of traveling on in front of the inferno, the smaller fire is pulled back toward it by the updrafts of the larger blaze. As it travels back to meet the large fire, the smaller backfire burns away the fuel that the forest fire needs to survive.

Even when a backfire has been well set, however, the fire may still win the struggle. The wind which the firefighters used to help them may now become their enemy. When the backfire meets the main fire, before both die for lack of fuel, there is tremendous flame, great heat and turbulent winds. A strong gust may blow the fire into the treetops beyond the area, giving the fire new fuel and a new life.

Main Idea	1		Answer	Score
		Mark the *main idea* ⟶	M	15
		Mark the statement that is *too broad* ⟶	B	5
		Mark the statement that is *too narrow* ⟶	N	5

a. A fire's own characteristics can be used to fight it. ☐ _____

b. Backfires are used to "fight fire with fire." ☐ _____

c. The heat of a fire can be useful as well as dangerous. ☐ _____

Score 15 points for each correct answer.   **Score**

Subject Matter **2** This passage focuses on
- ☐ a. how fires start.
- ☐ b. damage caused by fire.
- ☐ c. the fascination of fire.
- ☐ d. fighting forest fires.   _____

Supporting Details **3** A backfire is started
- ☐ a. behind a forest fire.
- ☐ b. ahead of a forest fire.
- ☐ c. on the sides of a forest fire.
- ☐ d. all around a forest fire.   _____

Conclusion **4** This passage suggests that a fire will travel
- ☐ a. faster than a horse can run.
- ☐ b. in all directions at the same speed.
- ☐ c. in whatever direction the wind is blowing.
- ☐ d. toward the nearest source of fuel.   _____

Clarifying Devices **5** In the last paragraph, the writer again refers to the fire as a living creature by saying that it
- ☐ a. can be blown around by the wind.
- ☐ b. dwarfs man's best efforts.
- ☐ c. heats the air above it.
- ☐ d. may still win the struggle.   _____

Vocabulary in Context **6** A turbulent wind
- ☐ a. blows in all directions.
- ☐ b. is extremely hot.
- ☐ c. circles like a tornado.
- ☐ d. has little strength.   _____

Add your scores for questions 1-6. Enter the total here and on the graph on page 239.   **Total Score** ☐

88

A Bird That Never Really Dies

The phoenix was one of the most magnificent birds that ever lived. Unfortunately for bird watchers, the grand phoenix lived only in the imaginations of the ancient Greeks and Egyptians.

According to Greek mythology, only one phoenix at a time lived on earth. The phoenix, a male, was brightly colored, with gold and red feathers. Legend has it that the single bird lived for exactly 500 years. Just before it was to die, it would build a nest. The mythical bird's last task was to sit patiently on the nest, waiting for the sun to ignite the dry twigs and set the nest ablaze. But as the proud phoenix sacrificed itself in flame, a tiny worm would crawl from beneath the ashes. This worm grew into a new phoenix. Its first task was to gather up its father's ashes and bury them in the temple of the Egyptian sun god in Heliopolis, the City of the Sun. Each reborn phoenix lived out the remainder of its life in Arabia.

Today, the phoenix symbolizes immortality. Also, someone who succeeds where he or she had previously failed is often referred to as a phoenix.

Main Idea	1		Answer	Score
		Mark the *main idea* ⟶	M	15
		Mark the statement that is *too broad* ⟶	B	5
		Mark the statement that is *too narrow* ⟶	N	5

a. Greek myths contain many stories of magical beasts and creatures. ☐ _____

b. The phoenix is a mythological bird that lived for 500 years and then sacrificed itself to give birth to a new phoenix. ☐ _____

c. A new phoenix was born from the ashes of the old phoenix. ☐ _____

Score 15 points for each correct answer.

Subject Matter   **2** This passage discusses an ancient
- ☐ a. king.
- ☐ b. myth.
- ☐ c. fairy tale.
- ☐ d. god.   _____

Supporting Details   **3** Most of a phoenix's life was supposedly spent in
- ☐ a. Greece.
- ☐ b. Egypt.
- ☐ c. Heliopolis.
- ☐ d. Arabia.   _____

Conclusion   **4** Someone who is called a phoenix today
- ☐ a. has come back from a defeat.
- ☐ b. is probably immortal.
- ☐ c. thinks he or she can live forever.
- ☐ d. is not well liked by colleagues.   _____

Clarifying Devices   **5** The life of the phoenix is described
- ☐ a. with the use of facts.
- ☐ b. in a humorous way.
- ☐ c. in an unclear way.
- ☐ d. step-by-step.   _____

Vocabulary in Context   **6** A person who is <u>immortal</u> could live
- ☐ a. for 800 years.
- ☐ b. forever.
- ☐ c. for 200 years.
- ☐ d. almost as long as the phoenix.   _____

Add your scores for questions 1-6. Enter the total here and on the graph on page 239.

Total Score ☐

Eye Facts

There are many commonly held beliefs about eyeglasses and eyesight that are not proven facts. For instance, some people believe that wearing glasses too soon weakens the eyes. But there is no evidence to show that the structure of eyes is changed by wearing glasses at a young age. Wearing the wrong glasses, however, can prove harmful. Studies show that for adults there is no danger, but children can <u>develop</u> loss of vision if they have the wrong glasses.

We have all heard some of the common myths about how eyesight gets bad. Most people believe that reading in dim light causes poor eyesight, but that is untrue. Too little light makes the eyes work harder, so they do get tired and strained. Eyestrain also results from reading a lot, reading in bed, and watching too much television. But, although eyestrain may cause some pain or headaches, it does not permanently damage eyesight.

Another myth about eyes is that they can be replaced, or transferred from one person to another. There are close to one million nerve fibers that connect the eyeball to the brain, and as of yet it is impossible to attach them all in a new person. Only certain parts of the eye—the cornea and the retina—can be replaced. But if we keep clearing up the myths and learning more about the eyes, someday a full transplant may be possible!

Main Idea	1		Answer	Score
	Mark the *main idea* ———→		M	15
	Mark the statement that is *too broad* ———→		B	5
	Mark the statement that is *too narrow* ———→		N	5

a. People have many false notions about eyes and sight. ☐ _____

b. There are many things about the body that are not completely understood. ☐ _____

c. There are several causes of eyestrain. ☐ _____

Score 15 points for each correct answer.　　　　　**Score**

Subject Matter

2 This passage is mostly about
- [ ] a. different types of eyeglasses.
- [ ] b. a visit to the eye doctor.
- [ ] c. myths about eyesight.
- [ ] d. cornea transplants.

_____

Supporting Details

3 One cause of eyestrain mentioned in the passage is
- [ ] a. wearing contact lenses too long.
- [ ] b. going to the movies.
- [ ] c. reading a lot.
- [ ] d. not visiting your eye doctor.

_____

Conclusion

4 From this passage one can conclude that
- [ ] a. doctors are still learning things about eyesight.
- [ ] b. headaches are only caused by eyestrain.
- [ ] c. everyone should wear glasses.
- [ ] d. people only believe things that are proven facts.

_____

Clarifying Devices

5 "Commonly held beliefs" are
- [ ] a. ideas that only low class people believe.
- [ ] b. ideas that most people believe.
- [ ] c. beliefs that have something in common.
- [ ] d. foolish beliefs.

_____

Vocabulary in Context

6 The word develop is used to mean
- [ ] a. become larger.
- [ ] b. create.
- [ ] c. train.
- [ ] d. acquire.

_____

Add your scores for questions 1-6. Enter the total here and on the graph on page 239.

Total Score ☐

The Giant Saguaro

The giant saguaro may well symbolize the desert, but it is more than a symbol, even more than a plant. To a host of creatures—birds, mammals and insects—the stately saguaro is home. It is an apartment house—and an air-conditioned one at that.

A pair of Gila woodpeckers constructed such an apartment atop a twenty-five-foot cactus. The carvers cut a hole two inches in diameter into the cactus. They bored straight in for about three inches, then turned sharply downward and dug a chamber about nine inches deep and four wide.

White pulp, exuding sticky sap, lined the hole. Over the next few months the sap hardened to form a dry, tough callus all around the hole, making the hard walls and a floor for the apartment. In April, the birds came back to move into their apartment and get started on the important business of raising babies. On the hard, bare floor of the hole, the lady laid four white eggs and sat on them in cool comfort.

Within the plant, behind the tough lining, the living sap of the cactus flowed. This liquid kept the temperature inside the hole well below the hot, midday temperature outside. All day the cactus absorbed heat from the sun, but the interior of the hole remained cooler than the sweltering outdoors. At night, when the outside heat quickly escaped into the sky, the woodpeckers were snug in their house, heated now by the warmed cactus sap.

Main Idea	1		Answer	Score
	Mark the *main idea*		M	15
	Mark the statement that is *too broad*		B	5
	Mark the statement that is *too narrow*		N	5

a. The saguaro cactus provides a cool, comfortable home for many animals. ☐ ____

b. The saguaro is a very useful plant. ☐ ____

c. The saguaro can become an air-conditioned apartment. ☐ ____

Score 15 points for each correct answer.   **Score**

Subject Matter

2 Another good title for this selection would be
- [ ] a. Woodpecker's Endurance.
- [ ] b. This Apartment Is for the Birds.
- [ ] c. Symbols of the Desert.
- [ ] d. Want to Buy a Cactus?   _____

Supporting Details

3 The hardened sap becomes the
- [ ] a. food for the young.
- [ ] b. air conditioning for the apartment.
- [ ] c. door of the apartment.
- [ ] d. walls and floor of the apartment.   _____

Conclusion

4 The author seems to admire the
- [ ] a. ideal suitability of the woodpecker's home.
- [ ] b. giant saguaro.
- [ ] c. desert's cruelty.
- [ ] d. intelligence of woodpeckers.   _____

Clarifying Devices

5 The author develops the main idea
- [ ] a. by showing contrasts.
- [ ] b. by using negative arguments.
- [ ] c. by describing an incident.
- [ ] d. by making a comparison.   _____

Vocabulary in Context

6 Sweltering means
- [ ] a. very dry.
- [ ] b. extremely hot.
- [ ] c. cruel.
- [ ] d. cold and icy.   _____

Add your scores for questions 1-6. Enter the total here and on the graph on page 239.   **Total Score** [ ]

91

Our Inner Senses

If we had to rely on only five senses for survival, we would be in very sad shape indeed. We wouldn't know up from down. We wouldn't know when to eat or drink. We wouldn't know what our muscles were doing or what position our limbs were in. We wouldn't know when our body was damaged, because we wouldn't feel pain. We might freeze to death without even a shiver, or overheat without a drop of sweat. The five senses—touch, taste, smell, hearing and sight—respond only to stimulation from the outside world, but the inside world of our bodies must also receive and respond to important messages.

Our internal senses keep us alive and enable us to use our external senses. In effect, the internal senses tell our brains how to run our bodies. Hunger and thirst <u>register</u> in a part of the brain called the hypothalamus, when a lack of food chemicals are detected in the blood.

Another internal sense that controls our balance is maintained by three fluid-filled loops in the inner ear. Changes in position and gravity affect the motion of this liquid and trigger changes in the brain. A sense called *kinesthesia* lets us know the relative positions of parts of our bodies. Even our breathing is triggered by a sense that identifies an over-abundance of carbon dioxide and a lack of oxygen in the blood.

No one has been able to count the number of internal senses. The presence of delicate internal senses shows just how marvelously complex we human beings are.

Main Idea	1		Answer	Score
		Mark the *main idea* ⟶	M	15
		Mark the statement that is *too broad* ⟶	B	5
		Mark the statement that is *too narrow* ⟶	N	5
		a. Many things are needed to make our bodies work right.	☐	____
		b. Our bodies are controlled by internal senses as well as by the five external senses.	☐	____
		c. The internal senses control balance and breathing.	☐	____

Score 15 points for each correct answer.   Score

Subject Matter **2** This passage deals mostly with the
- [ ] a. internal senses.
- [ ] b. sense of balance.
- [ ] c. five senses.
- [ ] d. brain's function.   _____

Supporting Details **3** Hunger is caused by
- [ ] a. too much food and water in the body.
- [ ] b. a lack of oxygen in the blood.
- [ ] c. seeing or thinking about food.
- [ ] d. a lack of certain chemicals in the blood.   _____

Conclusion **4** The passage implies that there are many senses we
- [ ] a. can use only in emergencies.
- [ ] b. may not understand at present.
- [ ] c. never realize we have.
- [ ] d. do not actively use in everyday living.   _____

Clarifying Devices **5** In the second paragraph, the term "in effect" means
- [ ] a. in fact.
- [ ] b. it is doubtful.
- [ ] c. without reason.
- [ ] d. often.   _____

Vocabulary in Context **6** Register, in this passage, most nearly means
- [ ] a. ignite.
- [ ] b. activate.
- [ ] c. signal.
- [ ] d. revise.   _____

Add your scores for questions 1-6. Enter the total here and on the graph on page 239.   Total ☐
Score

92

Bold Birds

It takes a bold bird to eat out of a person's hand. Pigeons do it all the time. But how about walking into a crocodile's mouth for your meal? Plovers, birds no bigger than a person's fist, regularly peck their meals out of the open jaws of live crocodiles!

Strangely enough, the tiny plover and the ferocious crocodile are trusting companions. Their friendly relationship is based on the fact that each animal provides a service for the other. After the crocodile has finished devouring a meal, it opens its powerful jaws and lets the little plover hop in. Once inside the threatening enclosure, the bird proceeds to pick the reptile's sharp teeth clean of uneaten food, with the crocodile's permission of course. In this way, the plover is rewarded with a filling meal in exchange for serving as the crocodile's toothbrush.

The plover also doubles as the crocodile's <u>groom</u> and lookout. As the crocodile moves along the river banks, the tiny bird rides on the reptile's back, pecking harmful parasites out of its host's rough hide. If another dangerous animal approaches the unlikely twosome, the little plover will let out shrill cries of warning from its moving perch.

Main Idea	1		Answer	Score
		Mark the *main idea* ⟶	M	15
		Mark the statement that is *too broad* ⟶	B	5
		Mark the statement that is *too narrow* ⟶	N	5

a. Plovers eat from the mouths of crocodiles. ☐ _____

b. Birds and crocodiles help each other. ☐ _____

c. Plovers and crocodiles help each other. ☐ _____

Subject Matter   **2**   The passage deals mostly with

☐ a. the eating habits of pigeons.

☐ b. the size of plovers.

☐ c. the relationship between plovers and crocodiles.

☐ d. the size of crocodiles' mouths.   _____

Supporting Details   **3**   One reason plovers ride on crocodiles' backs is

☐ a. because they can't fly.

☐ b. because they like the ride.

☐ c. to eat bugs from their hides.

☐ d. that they build their nests there.   _____

Conclusion   **4**   It is obvious from this passage that crocodiles

☐ a. are frightened of plovers.

☐ b. have no natural enemies.

☐ c. often eat plovers.

☐ d. do not eat plovers.   _____

Clarifying Devices   **5**   The writer develops the main idea of the passage by using

☐ a. arguments.

☐ b. contrasts.

☐ c. definitions.

☐ d. examples.   _____

Vocabulary in Context   **6**   In this passage <u>groom</u> means

☐ a. companion.

☐ b. personal cleaner.

☐ c. partner.

☐ d. navigator.   _____

Add your scores for questions 1-6. Enter the total here and on the graph on page 239.   **Total Score** ☐

93

The Ageless Wonder

When Bill Veeck, owner of the Cleveland Indians baseball team, signed aging Leroy "Satchel" Paige, Veeck was accused of doing it as a cheap publicity stunt. It was the sort of move a lot of people thought would be bad for the team and bad for baseball. Paige had been a legendary pitcher in the Negro Leagues, so what was the objection? His age.

Paige was always secretive about the date of his birth, but, at the time he was about to pitch his first major league game, most estimates put him at around forty-two years old. During his twenty years in the Negro Leagues, he had been the finest pitcher those leagues had ever seen. But the attitude in Cleveland was that he had been great in his day, but had surely outlived his effectiveness.

The night Paige played in his first game with Cleveland, 51,013 fans flocked into Comiskey Park in Chicago to see what the old man could do against the powerful White Sox. Satch was in complete control. He gave up only five hits, and the Indians beat the Sox 5-0. A week later Paige beat the Sox again in front of still another record-breaking crowd in the Indians' home stadium.

Veeck's faith in Paige had certainly been <u>vindicated</u>. The Indians won the American League Championship that year, and the contributions of the "Ageless Wonder," Satchel Paige, were responsible for a large part of their success.

Main Idea 1

	Answer	Score
Mark the *main idea* ⟶	M	15
Mark the statement that is *too broad* ⟶	B	5
Mark the statement that is *too narrow* ⟶	N	5

a. Despite his age, Paige proved to be an asset to the Cleveland Indians. ☐ _____

b. Many people thought Paige was too old to be in the Major Leagues. ☐ _____

c. Few people over forty play in the Major Leagues. ☐ _____

Score 15 points for each correct answer. Score

Subject Matter

2 The passage is mainly about
☐ a. the Negro League in baseball.
☐ b. Satchel Paige's early career.
☐ c. how Paige proved himself in the Majors.
☐ d. Paige's first game in the Majors. _____

Supporting Details

3 There was a crowd at Comiskey Park because
☐ a. Satchel Paige had never pitched before.
☐ b. Paige was very popular in Chicago.
☐ c. it was the American League playoffs.
☐ d. Satchel Paige was pitching for the first time in the Major Leagues. _____

Conclusion

4 The use of the phrase "cheap publicity stunt" to describe the signing of Paige by the Indians suggests that people believed
☐ a. Veeck didn't expect Paige to be good, but signed him to get publicity for the team.
☐ b. Bill Veeck didn't pay Paige very much.
☐ c. Paige wasn't really going to pitch, but was just going to be an attraction.
☐ d. publicity was all Paige cared about. _____

Clarifying Devices

5 The method used by the writer in the passage is
☐ a. logical argument.
☐ b. narration and description.
☐ c. questions and answers.
☐ d. exaggeration. _____

Vocabulary in Context

6 The best definition for the word <u>vindicated</u>, as used in the passage, is
☐ a. corrected.
☐ b. proved wrong.
☐ c. proved right.
☐ d. widely publicized. _____

Add your scores for questions 1–6. Enter the total here and on the graph on page 239. Total Score ☐

94

Supertree

It takes a long time to grow a tree. How long? Well, pine trees are the quickest growing trees, but still, they take twenty years to reach a size suitable for cutting and harvesting. An oak takes about sixty years to grow to a good size. A redwood may take hundreds of years.

Lumber companies, which make their money on trees, depend on those that grow quickly. Therefore, they are always looking for methods to make trees grow faster. So far, the secret to fast growing trees seems to lie in "superseeds." These are seeds that are gathered from the quickest growing trees in a forest. One company searched 100,000 acres of trees and selected the seeds from just fifteen trees. These two ounces of seed were enough to plant several hundred new trees. Eventually, when these trees have grown, seeds will again be taken only from the fastest growing trees of the crop. This process of artificial selection will yield, in the future, a supertree that will grow in half the time it takes normal trees to develop.

Unfortunately, it takes a long time for a plan like this to reach its goal. The Weyerhauser Lumber Corporation, which started its first collection of seed in 1958, is just now beginning to harvest the superseeds of the first generation of the faster growing trees.

Main Idea	1		Answer	Score
		Mark the *main idea* ⟶	M	15
		Mark the statement that is *too broad* ⟶	B	5
		Mark the statement that is *too narrow* ⟶	N	5

a. Fast growing trees are being developed to increase lumber production. ☐ _____

b. "Superseeds" will grow into trees that mature quickly. ☐ _____

c. Economic concerns of companies are often responsible for generating scientific experimentation. ☐ _____

Score 15 points for each correct answer.   **Score**

Subject   **2** This selection centers on
Matter
- [ ] a. the life span of trees.
- [ ] b. the age of redwoods.
- [ ] c. making trees grow quickly.
- [ ] d. cutting trees for lumber.   _____

Supporting **3** Trees that grow faster are developed by
Details
- [ ] a. planting many trees and fertilizing them.
- [ ] b. collecting seeds from strong, slow growing trees.
- [ ] c. selecting the seeds of the fastest growing trees.
- [ ] d. feeding them high-energy plant foods.   _____

Conclusion **4** Supertrees
- [ ] a. will be a great benefit to lumber companies.
- [ ] b. make extra-good lumber for buildings.
- [ ] c. will probably be weak because of their fast growth.
- [ ] d. may be vulnerable to many insects and diseases.   _____

Clarifying **5** The word *therefore* indicates that a
Devices
- [ ] a. speech is beginning.
- [ ] b. conclusion follows.
- [ ] c. comparison is being made.
- [ ] d. metaphor is being used.   _____

Vocabulary **6** In this passage <u>selection</u> means
in Context
- [ ] a. item.
- [ ] b. choice.
- [ ] c. passage.
- [ ] d. array.   _____

Add your scores for questions 1-6. Enter the   **Total**
total here and on the graph on page 239.   **Score** [   ]

95

Flying Tigers

Hawks and falcons are the wolves and tigers of the bird kingdom; they are meat-eaters that rely on strength and skill to catch their wary victims These birds have unusually good eyesight, great skill in flight, and sharp beaks and talons that quickly end the struggles of the animals they catch.

The hawks—a family that includes the bald eagle—tend to be large birds that hunt by soaring and gliding high in the air until they spot their prey on the ground. Then they drop down in a fast and accurate swoop, giving no warning until their wings flash open to break their fall, and their sharp talons close on their victims.

Falcons are usually smaller than hawks. They have long narrow wings designed for very fast flight. This family includes the peregrine falcon, called the bird of kings, which has been trained to hunt for the royalty of Europe and Africa for centuries. The peregrine, in its swoop upon its prey, has been <u>clocked</u> at speeds of over 100 miles per hour.

Hawks and falcons have suffered in recent years from people's war on insects. Small animals eat the insects that have been sprayed with chemicals, then these are eaten by larger animals that are in turn eaten by the birds of prey. The chemicals stay in the flesh of the animals. When the hawks have eaten a number of these animals, the chemicals have a deadly effect. The birds begin to lay eggs with very thin shells. The eggs break when the birds try to sit on them to keep them warm. So, no baby birds are hatched.

Main Idea	1		Answer	Score
	Mark the *main idea* ⟶	**M**	15
	Mark the statement that is *too broad* ⟶	**B**	5
	Mark the statement that is *too narrow* ⟶	**N**	5
	a. Hawks and falcons are powerful birds.	☐	
	b. Hawks and falcons survive by their great strength and skill.	☐	
	c. Hawks and falcons swoop down upon their prey.	☐	

**Subject
Matter**

2 Another good title for this selection would be

☐ a. The Rulers of the Skies.

☐ b. Bird Eaters.

☐ c. Wolves and Tigers.

☐ d. Beware of the Falcon.   _____

**Supporting
Details**

3 The chemicals that enter the bodies of hawks and falcons through the animals they eat eventually

☐ a. wear off and disappear.

☐ b. cause them to lay eggs with very thin shells.

☐ c. make them immune to diseases.

☐ d. cause them to die.   _____

Conclusion

4 From the passage, it appears that the writer

☐ a. thinks hawks and falcons are cruel.

☐ b. wants small animals to stop eating insects.

☐ c. objects to the spraying of chemicals on plants.

☐ d. wants to study the effects of chemicals.   _____

**Clarifying
Devices**

5 In the last sentence, *so* is used to mean

☐ a. "very."

☐ b. "so what."

☐ c. "in this way."

☐ d. "because of this."   _____

**Vocabulary
in Context**

6 Clocked, as used in this passage, means

☐ a. snapped.

☐ b. alarmed.

☐ c. timed.

☐ d. clicked.   _____

Add your scores for questions 1-6. Enter the total here and on the graph on page 239.   **Total Score** ☐

96

Living like a Lord

In 1829, the Earl of Bridgewater modified that age-old saying, "man's best friend is his dog." His version read, "man's best friends are his dogs."

The Earl of Bridgewater, also known as the Reverend Francis Henry Egerton, was not a silly man by any means. He was an accomplished scholar and a lover of fine art. Lord Egerton was also quite wealthy. But along with his more admirable qualities went Lord Egerton's obvious eccentricity.

It would be an understatement to say that Lord Egerton liked dogs. Lord Egerton, in fact, admired, respected and loved dogs.

Lord Egerton's permanent residence was a suite in the Hotel de Voailles in Paris, France. Each evening Lord Egerton sat down to an elegant dinner with ten or twelve of his favorite companions. The Reverend Egerton thoroughly enjoyed the company at his dinner table, though not much could be said for the conversation.

Each dinner guest was expected to conduct himself or herself with complete grace and dignity. After the meal, Lord Egerton and some of his guests would go for a ride in his private carriage. The guests were properly clothed with four boots each to keep their feet clean. Of course, two boots would not have been adequate for what were undoubtedly the best-dressed dogs in Paris.

Main Idea	1		Answer	Score
		Mark the *main idea* ⟶	M	15
		Mark the statement that is *too broad* ⟶	B	5
		Mark the statement that is *too narrow* ⟶	N	5

a. Lord Egerton ate dinner in the company of dogs. ☐ _____

b. Lord Egerton found dogs to be better company than people. ☐ _____

c. Lord Egerton had unusual companions. ☐ _____

Score 15 points for each correct answer.

Score

Subject Matter

2 The subject of this passage is
- [ ] a. a man's fondness for dogs.
- [ ] b. Parisian life.
- [ ] c. an elegant dinner in 1829.
- [ ] d. proper dog care.

_____

Supporting Details

3 Lord Egerton ate dinner in his
- [ ] a. castle.
- [ ] b. restaurant.
- [ ] c. hotel.
- [ ] d. house.

_____

Conclusion

4 It is obvious that Lord Egerton
- [ ] a. liked to eat.
- [ ] b. never ate with people.
- [ ] c. liked being wealthy.
- [ ] d. didn't enjoy the company of people very much.

_____

Clarifying Devices

5 The writer does a good job of
- [ ] a. fooling the reader.
- [ ] b. describing Lord Egerton's suite.
- [ ] c. arousing the reader's curiosity.
- [ ] d. describing nineteenth century Paris.

_____

Vocabulary in Context

6 <u>Eccentricity</u> is
- [ ] a. love of dogs.
- [ ] b. royal blood.
- [ ] c. insanity.
- [ ] d. odd behavior.

_____

Add your scores for questions 1-6. Enter the total here and on the graph on page 239.

Total Score ☐

215

97

Horse Sense

The crowd stirred and whispered in awe as, on the stage, the horse slowly tapped out the beat. Everyone became tense and quiet as the number of taps neared the correct answer to the horse trainer's question. After the final tap, the horse paused, seemed to look around and stopped. The crowd went wild!

The horse's name was *Clever Hans, the Educated Horse,* and was featured in a vaudeville act in the early 1900s, in Europe. When asked a complicated mathematical question by his owner, Clever Hans would tap out the correct answer with his hooves. For example, if the answer was sixty-eight, Hans would tap out six with his left hoof and eight with his right hoof. Even more remarkable, the owner would leave the room after asking the question, so there could be no secret signal between owner and horse. A mere animal seemed to be accomplishing a highly technical skill of man's!

It wasn't until years later that the secret of the trick was revealed. The owner had trained Clever Hans to respond to slight signals. The horse became so sensitive that he learned when to stop from the crowd's reaction. Members of the audience would <u>start</u> involuntarily, or give some unconscious signal, when Hans reached the right answer. Modern scientists now warn against the Clever Hans syndrome, whereby researchers unwittingly give clues to their animal subjects about the actions they would like to see performed!

Main Idea 1

	Answer	Score
Mark the *main idea* ⟶	**M**	15
Mark the statement that is *too broad* ⟶	**B**	5
Mark the statement that is *too narrow* ⟶	**N**	5

a. The horse, Clever Hans, was able to give correct answers to questions by reacting to audience clues. ☐ ____

b. Animals can be trained to do tricks that require sensitivity to audience reactions. ☐ ____

c. Clever Hans starred in his own vaudeville act. ☐ ____

Score 15 points for each correct answer. **Score**

Subject Matter

2 This passage is mainly about

☐ a. animal intelligence.

☐ b. mathematical skills.

☐ c. Clever Hans.

☐ d. unconscious behavior. _____

Supporting Details

3 The Clever Hans syndrome is a danger to be avoided by

☐ a. audiences.

☐ b. researchers.

☐ c. veterinarians.

☐ d. mathematicians. _____

Conclusion

4 Clever Hans's real talent was

☐ a. his sensitivity to crowd reactions.

☐ b. adding large sums.

☐ c. standing quietly on stage.

☐ d. obeying his owner. _____

Clarifying Devices

5 The first paragraph of this passage is

☐ a. a first person account.

☐ b. a dramatic account.

☐ c. an understatement.

☐ d. a scientific finding. _____

Vocabulary in Context

6 As used in this passage, the word start means

☐ a. cry out.

☐ b. begin.

☐ c. applaud.

☐ d. jerk. _____

Add your scores for questions 1-6. Enter the total here and on the graph on page 239. **Total Score** ☐

98

Animals Beware!

The history of executions is not a pleasant story. Executions that took place in the Middle Ages were especially bizarre. For example, many of the victims were animals. It was common for animals ranging from insects to wolves to be <u>tried</u> publicly. Ecclesiastical courts, which were courts that represented the church, would often decide that certain animals were witches or heretics. The court's punishment was often excommunication (expulsion from the church), torture or death. One of the last animal executions took place in France, in 1740. The presiding judge ordered that a cow be hung by its neck because he believed it to be a sorcerer.

One of the most striking stories recorded concerned a pig that lived 600 years ago. This pig had killed a little girl—or at least this is what the judge was told. For its crime, the pig was to have its legs mutilated, and then it was to be hanged. In preparation for this grisly end, the pig was dressed up in a child's jacket and ceremoniously dragged into the public square. The execution was called a "six sous" job because the executioner was given six French sous, or pennies, to buy a pair of gloves in order to keep his hands clean during the execution.

Main Idea	1		Answer	Score
	Mark the *main idea* ⟶	M		15
	Mark the statement that is *too broad* ⟶	B		5
	Mark the statement that is *too narrow* ⟶	N		5

a. In the Middle Ages, pigs were tried for crimes. ☐ _____

b. Killing animals was common during the Middle Ages. ☐ _____

c. Centuries ago, animals were often tried and executed. ☐ _____

Score 15 points for each correct answer.   **Score**

Subject Matter

2 The subject of the passage is

☐ a. animals.
☐ b. animal executions.
☐ c. hangings.
☐ d. the Middle Ages.   _____

Supporting Details

3 Six hundred years ago, people believed that animals could commit

☐ a. larceny.
☐ b. adultery.
☐ c. robbery.
☐ d. murder.   _____

Conclusion

4 It is obvious that many people of the past were

☐ a. unhappy.
☐ b. peaceful.
☐ c. superstitious.
☐ d. angry.   _____

Clarifying Devices

5 The phrase "One of the most striking stories" is an indication that the story that follows will be

☐ a. very difficult.
☐ b. especially surprising.
☐ c. hard to take.
☐ d. very beautiful.   _____

Vocabulary in Context

6 In this passage <u>tried</u> means

☐ a. given a trial.
☐ b. given a hard time.
☐ c. saw how it worked.
☐ d. melted for fat.   _____

Add your scores for questions 1-6. Enter the total here and on the graph on page 239.

Total Score ☐

99

The Roadrunner

The Roadrunner of cartoon fame is patterned after a real bird that is the state bird of New Mexico and a member of the cuckoo family. The real roadrunner is about twenty inches long and has a strong, versatile tail that is almost as long as its body. Its name comes from the peculiar habit that it had of running ahead of horses and carriages in the days of the Old West. The roadrunner's powerful legs propel it at speeds of up to twenty miles per hour, while its extra-long tail helps it keep its balance. Although the bird can fly with ease, it prefers to stay on the ground, depending on its remarkable agility to escape unfriendly coyotes and other predators.

Since it lives in the desert, the roadrunner feeds on snakes, lizards, large insects and snails. The bird will sometimes surprise and kill a rattlesnake by pecking at it and dodging its strikes until the snake is too tired to move. The brown bird then picks up the snake and dashes it against the ground, killing it. Occasionally, the roadrunner goes into high gear to chase rabbits, but not to harm them. Instead, it snaps up insects disturbed by the rabbit's run. Taking twenty steps a second and moving at twenty miles per hour, this speedy bird eats the jumping and flying insects without missing a beep-beep.

Main Idea	1		Answer	Score
	Mark the *main idea* →		M	15
	Mark the statement that is *too broad* →		B	5
	Mark the statement that is *too narrow* →		N	5

a. The birds of New Mexico are fast runners. ☐ ____

b. The roadrunner is a very fast and agile desert bird. ☐ ____

c. The roadrunner depends on its speed for protection. ☐ ____

Score 15 points for each correct answer.

Subject Matter

2 This passage is mostly about
- ☐ a. a cartoon.
- ☐ b. a wily coyote.
- ☐ c. the roadrunner.
- ☐ d. how birds kill snakes. _____

Supporting Details

3 The roadrunner runs on the ground because it
- ☐ a. doesn't have wings.
- ☐ b. has long legs.
- ☐ c. doesn't like to fly.
- ☐ d. looks for animal tracks. _____

Conclusion

4 We can conclude from this passage that
- ☐ a. coyotes are a favorite snack for the bird.
- ☐ b. the roadrunner depends on speed for survival.
- ☐ c. snakes ignore roadrunners.
- ☐ d. roadrunners have no natural enemies. _____

Clarifying Devices

5 The word *although* in the first paragraph signals
- ☐ a. two related ideas.
- ☐ b. the beginning of a sentence.
- ☐ c. an argument.
- ☐ d. some logical reasoning. _____

Vocabulary in Context

6 Propel means
- ☐ a. cause to fly.
- ☐ b. wind up.
- ☐ c. push forward.
- ☐ d. lift. _____

Add your scores for questions 1-6. Enter the total here and on the graph on page 239.

Total Score ☐

100

Rags to Riches

He found success, but not without a fight. A man named John Gully, born in England in 1773, fought his way from prison to several terms in the House of Commons—literally!

Gully was in debtor's prison, a jail for people who can't pay the money they owe. In 1805, the heavyweight boxing champion of England, Henry Pierce, visited the prison to entertain the inmates. Gully was chosen to fight against Pierce. It should have been an easy victory for the champion. Instead, Gully soundly defeated him!

The story of the fight reached the ears of several gamblers. They pooled their resources and paid off Gully's debts. In return, he was to fight for them in exhibition matches. Gully won every fight. In fact, he saved enough money to buy himself out of the deal he had made with the men.

A year later he fought Pierce again. This time it was the official match for the national championship. Gully was beaten for the first and last time in his career, but he had held his own for fifty-nine rounds! He finally did become champion in 1807, when Pierce died.

When he had accrued a small fortune, Gully invested it in horse racing. He gave up boxing. Two of his race horses won the English Derby.

By 1832 he was wealthy and respectable enough to run for a seat in Parliament. He was elected to the House of Commons for several terms before he died in 1863, at the age of 90.

Main Idea	1		Answer	Score
	Mark the *main idea* ⟶		M	15
	Mark the statement that is *too broad* ⟶		B	5
	Mark the statement that is *too narrow* ⟶		N	5
	a. John Gully was a good fighter.		☐	
	b. By working hard, one can overcome high odds.		☐	
	c. John Gully managed to attain a higher position in life through perseverance.		☐	

Score 15 points for each correct answer.

Subject Matter **2** This passage deals with
- ☐ a. the British Parliament.
- ☐ b. a man's rise from bankruptcy to honor and wealth.
- ☐ c. a battle for a boxing championship.
- ☐ d. a popular men's sport in nineteenth century England. _____

Supporting Details **3** Gully became national champion when
- ☐ a. his last match with Pierce ended in victory.
- ☐ b. Pierce defaulted to him.
- ☐ c. the former champion died.
- ☐ d. his horses won the English Derby. _____

Conclusion **4** We can assume from the passage that Gully
- ☐ a. was an ambitious man.
- ☐ b. was never really respectable.
- ☐ c. never liked to fight.
- ☐ d. hated Pierce for beating him. _____

Clarifying Devices **5** The way in which the writer presents the story makes the reader feel that the success of John Gully was
- ☐ a. pure luck.
- ☐ b. faked.
- ☐ c. undeserved.
- ☐ d. well-earned. _____

Vocabulary in Context **6** <u>Match</u>, in this passage, means
- ☐ a. fire stick.
- ☐ b. contest.
- ☐ c. two things that go well together.
- ☐ d. pair up. _____

Add your scores for questions 1-6. Enter the total here and on the graph on page 239.

Total Score ☐

Answer Key

Passage 1:	1a. **M**	1b. **N**	1c. **B**	2. **b**	3. **b**	4. **c**	5. **d**	6. **c**
Passage 2:	1a. **M**	1b. **N**	1c. **B**	2. **b**	3. **d**	4. **d**	5. **c**	6. **b**
Passage 3:	1a. **B**	1b. **N**	1c. **M**	2. **a**	3. **b**	4. **d**	5. **b**	6. **d**
Passage 4:	1a. **M**	1b. **B**	1c. **N**	2. **b**	3. **a**	4. **c**	5. **c**	6. **c**
Passage 5:	1a. **M**	1b. **B**	1c. **N**	2. **b**	3. **c**	4. **a**	5. **b**	6. **a**
Passage 6:	1a. **N**	1b. **M**	1c. **B**	2. **c**	3. **d**	4. **a**	5. **c**	6. **b**
Passage 7:	1a. **N**	1b. **B**	1c. **M**	2. **b**	3. **c**	4. **a**	5. **b**	6. **d**
Passage 8:	1a. **N**	1b. **B**	1c. **M**	2. **c**	3. **a**	4. **b**	5. **c**	6. **b**
Passage 9:	1a. **N**	1b. **M**	1c. **B**	2. **b**	3. **d**	4. **a**	5. **c**	6. **b**
Passage 10:	1a. **B**	1b. **M**	1c. **N**	2. **c**	3. **d**	4. **c**	5. **b**	6. **a**
Passage 11:	1a. **N**	1b. **B**	1c. **M**	2. **c**	3. **a**	4. **d**	5. **d**	6. **b**
Passage 12:	1a. **M**	1b. **B**	1c. **N**	2. **c**	3. **a**	4. **b**	5. **b**	6. **b**
Passage 13:	1a. **B**	1b. **M**	1c. **N**	2. **c**	3. **d**	4. **b**	5. **a**	6. **c**
Passage 14:	1a. **B**	1b. **M**	1c. **N**	2. **c**	3. **b**	4. **a**	5. **c**	6. **a**
Passage 15:	1a. **N**	1b. **B**	1c. **M**	2. **c**	3. **b**	4. **d**	5. **b**	6. **c**
Passage 16:	1a. **B**	1b. **M**	1c. **N**	2. **d**	3. **a**	4. **c**	5. **b**	6. **c**
Passage 17:	1a. **N**	1b. **M**	1c. **B**	2. **a**	3. **b**	4. **d**	5. **a**	6. **a**
Passage 18:	1a. **N**	1b. **M**	1c. **B**	2. **b**	3. **c**	4. **d**	5. **b**	6. **b**
Passage 19:	1a. **N**	1b. **B**	1c. **M**	2. **c**	3. **c**	4. **b**	5. **c**	6. **c**
Passage 20:	1a. **M**	1b. **N**	1c. **B**	2. **c**	3. **c**	4. **c**	5. **c**	6. **b**

Passage 21:	1a. **M**	1b. **N**	1c. **B**	2. b	3. c	4. c	5. a	6. c
Passage 22:	1a. **B**	1b. **M**	1c. **N**	2. a	3. c	4. c	5. b	6. c
Passage 23:	1a. **M**	1b. **B**	1c. **N**	2. b	3. d	4. c	5. a	6. d
Passage 24:	1a. **N**	1b. **M**	1c. **B**	2. b	3. d	4. a	5. c	6. b
Passage 25:	1a. **B**	1b. **M**	1c. **N**	2. b	3. a	4. c	5. c	6. b
Passage 26:	1a. **M**	1b. **N**	1c. **B**	2. d	3. d	4. a	5. c	6. a
Passage 27:	1a. **B**	1b. **M**	1c. **N**	2. c	3. a	4. c	5. a	6. b
Passage 28:	1a. **M**	1b. **N**	1c. **B**	2. b	3. d	4. b	5. d	6. c
Passage 29:	1a. **N**	1b. **M**	1c. **B**	2. a	3. c	4. d	5. a	6. a
Passage 30:	1a. **B**	1b. **M**	1c. **N**	2. b	3. d	4. a	5. c	6. c
Passage 31:	1a. **B**	1b. **N**	1c. **M**	2. a	3. c	4. c	5. b	6. c
Passage 32:	1a. **B**	1b. **N**	1c. **M**	2. b	3. b	4. d	5. c	6. c
Passage 33:	1a. **N**	1b. **M**	1c. **B**	2. d	3. c	4. a	5. b	6. d
Passage 34:	1a. **B**	1b. **M**	1c. **N**	2. c	3. a	4. d	5. c	6. b
Passage 35:	1a. **M**	1b. **B**	1c. **N**	2. b	3. c	4. b	5. a	6. c
Passage 36:	1a. **M**	1b. **B**	1c. **N**	2. c	3. d	4. b	5. c	6. b
Passage 37:	1a. **B**	1b. **N**	1c. **M**	2. d	3. a	4. b	5. d	6. c
Passage 38:	1a. **N**	1b. **B**	1c. **M**	2. c	3. a	4. c	5. d	6. c
Passage 39:	1a. **N**	1b. **B**	1c. **M**	2. c	3. c	4. c	5. c	6. a
Passage 40:	1a. **M**	1b. **B**	1c. **N**	2. b	3. c	4. b	5. c	6. d

Passage 41:	1a. **N**	1b. **M**	1c. **B**	2. **b**	3. **c**	4. **a**	5. **b**	6. **d**
Passage 42:	1a. **B**	1b. **M**	1c. **N**	2. **c**	3. **b**	4. **c**	5. **a**	6. **c**
Passage 43:	1a. **B**	1b. **M**	1c. **N**	2. **c**	3. **d**	4. **b**	5. **d**	6. **b**
Passage 44:	1a. **B**	1b. **M**	1c. **N**	2. **b**	3. **c**	4. **b**	5. **d**	6. **a**
Passage 45:	1a. **M**	1b. **N**	1c. **B**	2. **a**	3. **d**	4. **b**	5. **c**	6. **c**
Passage 46:	1a. **M**	1b. **B**	1c. **N**	2. **b**	3. **c**	4. **c**	5. **a**	6. **c**
Passage 47:	1a. **N**	1b. **M**	1c. **B**	2. **a**	3. **d**	4. **b**	5. **c**	6. **c**
Passage 48:	1a. **N**	1b. **B**	1c. **M**	2. **d**	3. **c**	4. **d**	5. **a**	6. **c**
Passage 49:	1a. **N**	1b. **M**	1c. **B**	2. **c**	3. **d**	4. **a**	5. **a**	6. **b**
Passage 50:	1a. **M**	1b. **N**	1c. **B**	2. **c**	3. **b**	4. **b**	5. **a**	6. **b**
Passage 51:	1a. **B**	1b. **M**	1c. **N**	2. **c**	3. **d**	4. **b**	5. **a**	6. **b**
Passage 52:	1a. **B**	1b. **M**	1c. **N**	2. **a**	3. **c**	4. **c**	5. **c**	6. **b**
Passage 53:	1a. **M**	1b. **N**	1c. **B**	2. **d**	3. **c**	4. **d**	5. **b**	6. **c**
Passage 54:	1a. **M**	1b. **N**	1c. **B**	2. **b**	3. **d**	4. **c**	5. **c**	6. **b**
Passage 55:	1a. **B**	1b. **M**	1c. **N**	2. **a**	3. **b**	4. **a**	5. **a**	6. **a**
Passage 56:	1a. **N**	1b. **M**	1c. **B**	2. **a**	3. **c**	4. **c**	5. **b**	6. **d**
Passage 57:	1a. **B**	1b. **N**	1c. **M**	2. **c**	3. **c**	4. **c**	5. **a**	6. **c**
Passage 58:	1a. **B**	1b. **N**	1c. **M**	2. **c**	3. **d**	4. **a**	5. **b**	6. **c**
Passage 59:	1a. **M**	1b. **B**	1c. **N**	2. **b**	3. **b**	4. **c**	5. **a**	6. **d**
Passage 60:	1a. **M**	1b. **B**	1c. **N**	2. **b**	3. **c**	4. **c**	5. **a**	6. **c**

Passage 61:	1a. **B**	1b. **M**	1c. **N**	2. **b**	3. **b**	4. **c**	5. **a**	6. **b**
Passage 62:	1a. **B**	1b. **M**	1c. **N**	2. **b**	3. **d**	4. **c**	5. **d**	6. **b**
Passage 63:	1a. **M**	1b. **B**	1c. **N**	2. **b**	3. **c**	4. **c**	5. **b**	6. **b**
Passage 64:	1a. **M**	1b. **B**	1c. **N**	2. **c**	3. **d**	4. **b**	5. **c**	6. **c**
Passage 65:	1a. **N**	1b. **M**	1c. **B**	2. **d**	3. **c**	4. **d**	5. **a**	6. **c**
Passage 66:	1a. **M**	1b. **B**	1c. **N**	2. **c**	3. **b**	4. **c**	5. **a**	6. **b**
Passage 67:	1a. **B**	1b. **N**	1c. **M**	2. **b**	3. **a**	4. **a**	5. **b**	6. **d**
Passage 68:	1a. **B**	1b. **N**	1c. **M**	2. **b**	3. **b**	4. **c**	5. **b**	6. **b**
Passage 69:	1a. **M**	1b. **N**	1c. **B**	2. **b**	3. **d**	4. **d**	5. **c**	6. **b**
Passage 70:	1a. **N**	1b. **M**	1c. **B**	2. **c**	3. **d**	4. **c**	5. **d**	6. **c**
Passage 71:	1a. **N**	1b. **B**	1c. **M**	2. **c**	3. **b**	4. **d**	5. **a**	6. **c**
Passage 72:	1a. **B**	1b. **M**	1c. **N**	2. **d**	3. **c**	4. **c**	5. **b**	6. **d**
Passage 73:	1a. **M**	1b. **N**	1c. **B**	2. **c**	3. **b**	4. **d**	5. **a**	6. **c**
Passage 74:	1a. **M**	1b. **B**	1c. **N**	2. **c**	3. **d**	4. **a**	5. **a**	6. **c**
Passage 75:	1a. **M**	1b. **B**	1c. **N**	2. **d**	3. **a**	4. **d**	5. **d**	6. **b**
Passage 76:	1a. **M**	1b. **B**	1c. **N**	2. **b**	3. **a**	4. **c**	5. **c**	6. **d**
Passage 77:	1a. **B**	1b. **N**	1c. **M**	2. **c**	3. **c**	4. **b**	5. **c**	6. **a**
Passage 78:	1a. **M**	1b. **N**	1c. **B**	2. **d**	3. **d**	4. **c**	5. **b**	6. **b**
Passage 79:	1a. **B**	1b. **N**	1c. **M**	2. **b**	3. **d**	4. **a**	5. **c**	6. **c**
Passage 80:	1a. **M**	1b. **B**	1c. **N**	2. **b**	3. **b**	4. **c**	5. **a**	6. **c**

Passage 81:	1a. **M**	1b. **B**	1c. **N**	2. **b**	3. c	4. **a**	5. **d**	6. c
Passage 82:	1a. **M**	1b. **N**	1c. **B**	2. **d**	3. c	4. b	5. a	6. **d**
Passage 83:	1a. **B**	1b. **M**	1c. **N**	2. **b**	3. a	4. b	5. **d**	6. a
Passage 84:	1a. **M**	1b. **B**	1c. **N**	2. **b**	3. **d**	4. b	5. c	6. **d**
Passage 85:	1a. **M**	1b. **N**	1c. **B**	2. c	3. **b**	4. c	5. a	6. **d**
Passage 86:	1a. **N**	1b. **B**	1c. **M**	2. c	3. c	4. b	5. a	6. **d**
Passage 87:	1a. **M**	1b. **N**	1c. **B**	2. **d**	3. **b**	4. c	5. **d**	6. a
Passage 88:	1a. **B**	1b. **M**	1c. **N**	2. **b**	3. **d**	4. **a**	5. **d**	6. **b**
Passage 89:	1a. **M**	1b. **B**	1c. **N**	2. c	3. c	4. **a**	5. **b**	6. **d**
Passage 90:	1a. **M**	1b. **B**	1c. **N**	2. **b**	3. **d**	4. **a**	5. c	6. **b**
Passage 91:	1a. **B**	1b. **M**	1c. **N**	2. **a**	3. **d**	4. c	5. a	6. c
Passage 92:	1a. **N**	1b. **B**	1c. **M**	2. c	3. c	4. **d**	5. **d**	6. **b**
Passage 93:	1a. **M**	1b. **N**	1c. **B**	2. c	3. **d**	4. **a**	5. **b**	6. c
Passage 94:	1a. **M**	1b. **N**	1c. **B**	2. c	3. c	4. **a**	5. **b**	6. **b**
Passage 95:	1a. **B**	1b. **M**	1c. **N**	2. **a**	3. **b**	4. c	5. **d**	6. c
Passage 96:	1a. **N**	1b. **M**	1c. **B**	2. **a**	3. c	4. **d**	5. c	6. **d**
Passage 97:	1a. **M**	1b. **B**	1c. **N**	2. c	3. **b**	4. **a**	5. **b**	6. **d**
Passage 98:	1a. **N**	1b. **B**	1c. **M**	2. **b**	3. **d**	4. c	5. **b**	6. a
Passage 99:	1a. **B**	1b. **M**	1c. **N**	2. c	3. c	4. b	5. a	6. c
Passage 100:	1a. **N**	1b. **B**	1c. **M**	2. **b**	3. c	4. **a**	5. **d**	6. **b**

Diagnostic Chart (For Student Correction)

Directions: For each passage, write your answers to the *left* of the dotted line in the blocks for each skill category. Then correct your answers using the Answer Key on page 225. If your answer is correct, do not make any more marks in the block. If your answer is incorrect, write the letter of the correct answer to the *right* of the dotted line.

	Categories of Comprehension Skills								
	1 Main Idea			Subject Matter	2 Supporting Details	3 Conclusion	4 Clarifying Devices	5 Vocabulary in Context	6
	Statement a	Statement b	Statement c						
Passage 1									
Passage 2									
Passage 3									
Passage 4									
Passage 5									
Passage 6									
Passage 7									
Passage 8									
Passage 9									
Passage 10									
Passage 11									
Passage 12									
Passage 13									
Passage 14									
Passage 15									
Passage 16									
Passage 17									
Passage 18									
Passage 19									
Passage 20									

Directions: For each passage, write your answers to the *left* of the dotted line in the blocks for each skill category. Then correct your answers using the Answer Key on page 226. If your answer is correct, do not make any more marks in the block. If your answer is incorrect, write the letter of the correct answer to the *right* of the dotted line.

	Categories of Comprehension Skills								
	1 Main Idea				2	3	4	5	6
	Statement a	Statement b	Statement c	Subject Matter	Supporting Details	Conclusion	Clarifying Devices	Vocabulary in Context	
Passage 21									
Passage 22									
Passage 23									
Passage 24									
Passage 25									
Passage 26									
Passage 27									
Passage 28									
Passage 29									
Passage 30									
Passage 31									
Passage 32									
Passage 33									
Passage 34									
Passage 35									
Passage 36									
Passage 37									
Passage 38									
Passage 39									
Passage 40									

Directions: For each passage, write your answers to the *left* of the dotted line in the blocks for each skill category. Then correct your answers using the Answer Key on page 227. If your answer is correct, do not make any more marks in the block. If your answer is incorrect, write the letter of the correct answer to the *right* of the dotted line.

	Categories of Comprehension Skills								
	1 Main Idea			Subject Matter	2 Supporting Details	3 Conclusion	4 Clarifying Devices	5 Vocabulary in Context	6
	Statement a	Statement b	Statement c						
Passage 41									
Passage 42									
Passage 43									
Passage 44									
Passage 45									
Passage 46									
Passage 47									
Passage 48									
Passage 49									
Passage 50									
Passage 51									
Passage 52									
Passage 53									
Passage 54									
Passage 55									
Passage 56									
Passage 57									
Passage 58									
Passage 59									
Passage 60									

Directions: For each passage, write your answers to the *left* of the dotted line in the blocks for each skill category. Then correct your answers using the Answer Key on page 228. If your answer is correct, do not make any more marks in the block. If your answer is incorrect, write the letter of the correct answer to the *right* of the dotted line.

	Categories of Comprehension Skills								
	1 Main Idea				2	3	4	5	6
	Statement a	Statement b	Statement c	Subject Matter	Supporting Details	Conclusion	Clarifying Devices	Vocabulary in Context	
Passage 61									
Passage 62									
Passage 63									
Passage 64									
Passage 65									
Passage 66									
Passage 67									
Passage 68									
Passage 69									
Passage 70									
Passage 71									
Passage 72									
Passage 73									
Passage 74									
Passage 75									
Passage 76									
Passage 77									
Passage 78									
Passage 79									
Passage 80									

Directions: For each passage, write your answers to the *left* of the dotted line in the blocks for each skill category. Then correct your answers using the Answer Key on page 229. If your answer is correct, do not make any more marks in the block. If your answer is incorrect, write the letter of the correct answer to the *right* of the dotted line.

	Categories of Comprehension Skills							
	1 Main Idea			2	3	4	5	6
	Statement a	Statement b	Statement c	Subject Matter	Supporting Details	Conclusion	Clarifying Devices	Vocabulary in Context
Passage 81								
Passage 82								
Passage 83								
Passage 84								
Passage 85								
Passage 86								
Passage 87								
Passage 88								
Passage 89								
Passage 90								
Passage 91								
Passage 92								
Passage 93								
Passage 94								
Passage 95								
Passage 96								
Passage 97								
Passage 98								
Passage 99								
Passage 100								

Progress Graph

Directions: Write your Total Score for each passage in the comprehension score box under the number of the passage. Then plot your score on the graph itself by putting a small **x** on the line directly above the number of the passage, across from the score you got for that passage. As you mark your score for each passage, graph your progress by drawing a line to connect the **x**'s.

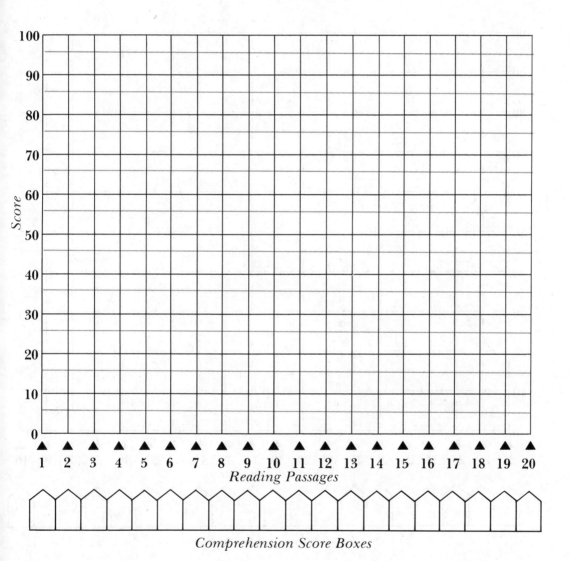

Comprehension Score Boxes

Directions: Write your Total Score for each passage in the comprehension score box under the number of the passage. Then plot your score on the graph itself by putting a small **x** on the line directly above the number of the passage, across from the score you got for that passage. As you mark your score for each passage, graph your progress by drawing a line to connect the **x**'s.

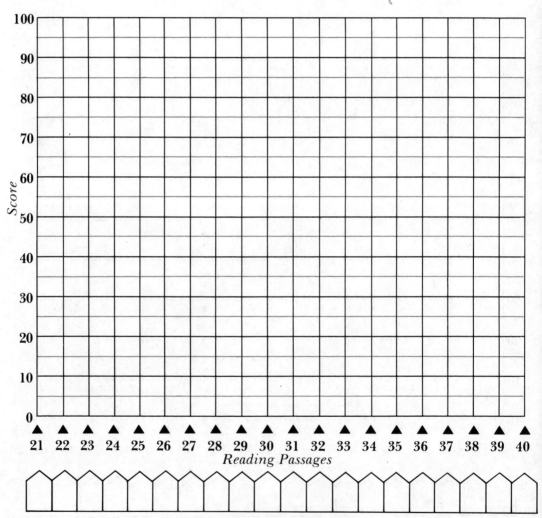

Reading Passages

Comprehension Score Boxes

Directions: Write your Total Score for each passage in the comprehension score box under the number of the passage. Then plot your score on the graph itself by putting a small **x** on the line directly above the number of the passage, across from the score you got for that passage. As you mark your score for each passage, graph your progress by drawing a line to connect the **x**'s.

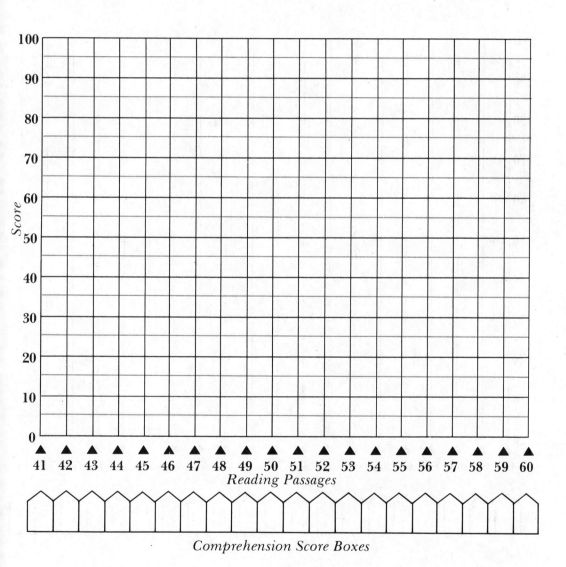

Reading Passages

Comprehension Score Boxes

Directions: Write your Total Score for each passage in the comprehension score box under the number of the passage. Then plot your score on the graph itself by putting a small **x** on the line directly above the number of the passage, across from the score you got for that passage. As you mark your score for each passage, graph your progress by drawing a line to connect the **x**'s.

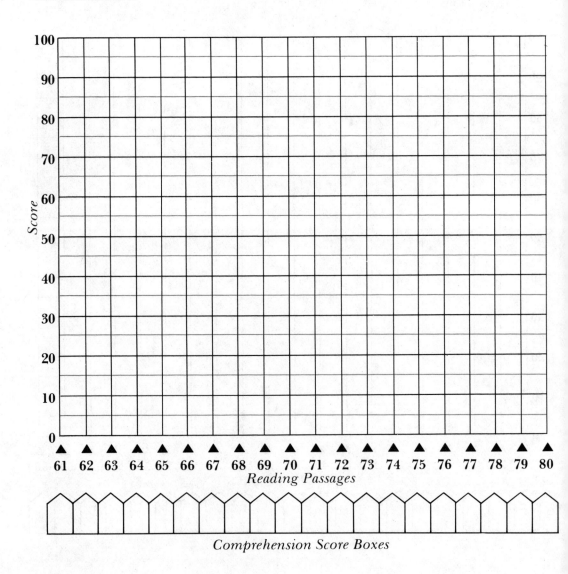

Reading Passages

Comprehension Score Boxes

Directions: Write your Total Score for each passage in the comprehension score box under the number of the passage. Then plot your score on the graph itself by putting a small **x** on the line directly above the number of the passage, across from the score you got for that passage. As you mark your score for each passage, graph your progress by drawing a line to connect the **x**'s.

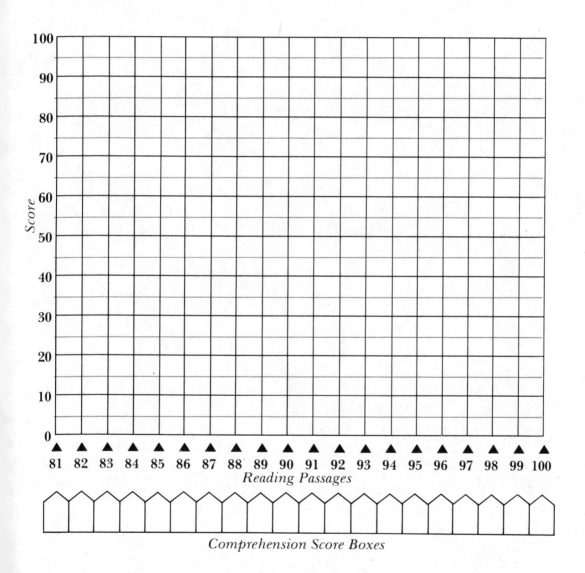

Reading Passages

Comprehension Score Boxes